MAGNA MINDSET

THE ELITE MINDSET OF WORLD-CLASS PRODUCERS

BRUCE DANIELSON

Copyright © 2025 by Bruce Danielson
Published by Magna Mindset Training System

This book or any portion thereof may not be reproduced or used in any manner whatsoever without the express written permission of the publisher except for the use of brief quotations in a book review.

All rights reserved.

ISBN 13: 979-8-218-75069-5

Cover design: L. Douglas Hogan

For more information visit:
https://magnamindsettraining.com

CONTENTS

Acknowledgements	v
Foreword	ix
Preface	xi
What This Book Is About	xv
Performance Goals and Objectives	xix

1. **Evaluate Your Mindset** — 1
   What Mental Operating System Runs Your Performance?
2. **Resistance, Fear, and Failure** — 29
   Where Your Greatest Strengths Lie Waiting to Be Unleashed
3. **World-Class Mental Toughness** — 41
   The Driving Force Behind Transformation and Growth
4. **World-Class Attitude** — 55
   The Operating System of Elite Performance
5. **World-Class Emotional Intelligence** — 73
   Emotions Aren't Obstacles—They're Operating Instructions
6. **World-Class Responsibility** — 93
   The Architecture of Accountability That Shapes Performance
7. **The Power of NOW** — 105
   The Art of Relentless Presence
8. **Authentic Enthusiasm** — 115
   Expressing Belief, Not Performing Emotion
9. **The Death Stars of Our Emotions - The 3 R's** — 123
   Emotional Saboteurs of Performance
10. **Magna Mindset Overview** — 143
    "Elite Isn't a Personality, It's a Practice" - Bruce Danielson

The Final Transformation of Your Mindset	147
About the Author	149

ACKNOWLEDGEMENTS

This book and the philosophy within it would not have come to life without the insight, support, and inspiration of a few extraordinary people.

To Al Batinga, thank you for seeing the possibility before it was even on paper. Your encouragement to write about elite performance gave me the push to pursue depth, discipline, and clarity in how mindset transforms lives.

To Keith Cupp, your strategic brain and generous guidance helped me carve out the framework behind the *Magna Mindset* philosophy. From foundational insight to digital design, your influence is embedded in every layer of this work.

To my brilliant wife, Michelle, you've taught me more about language, grace, and emotional clarity than any textbook ever could. Your love and patience throughout the process, especially as I refined my writing voice, grounded me in strength and humility. This book carries your fingerprints.

ACKNOWLEDGEMENTS

To my two exceptional children, Stephen and Annie, you are my living, breathing reminders of adventure and authenticity. Watching you engage with life boldly and uniquely has inspired me far more than you know. You continue to teach me how to lead with heart, curiosity, and real presence. I love you always. — *Dad*

And to G. Michael Hopf at *Beyond the Fray Publishing*, your knowledge, guidance, and passion for this book were invaluable. I couldn't have asked for more. Your belief in this project made the publishing journey not just possible, but meaningful.

Mind-set (noun) -

Habitual Mental Attitude That Determines How You Will Interpret and Respond to Various Situations

Our life is what our thoughts make it – Marcus Aurelius

FOREWORD

I'm thrilled to introduce *Magna Mindset - The Elite Mindset of World-Class Producers* - a book that captures the mental strategies needed to dominate in sales and life.

I've known Bruce for over 20 years, first as his General Manager at New Horizons Computer Learning Center and later as President, where he served as a National Senior Sales Executive and consistently ranked in the top 1% among hundreds of salespeople. Bruce's ability to outperform wasn't just talent—it was his unshakeable mindset. He's maintained that elite status across industries, from tech training at New Horizons to Insurance and Financial Services, proving his approach works.

Magna Mindset - isn't just another self-help book; it's a battle-tested guide to building the emotional and psychological development of mental toughness, emotional intelligence, attitude and responsibility in becoming an elite producer. In today's rapidly evolving sales landscape, where digital tools like social media and CRM platforms are essential, the foundation of success remains the same: a powerful mindset. *Magna Mindset* equips you with the mental strategies to thrive in any sales environment, from navigating new technologies to leveraging years of experience. Bruce's strategies help you perform above the grind of sales with personal well-being, ensuring you thrive both professionally and personally. Research shows that salespeople with a growth mindset consistently outperform those with a fixed mindset, and *Magna Mindset* provides the tools to cultivate that winning attitude.

If you're serious about taking your sales career to the next level and I mean *truly* serious, grab this book now. Don't just read it, act on it. Start today by evaluating your mindset and applying the principles and strategies elite producers use. As someone who has trained organizations from startups to Fortune 500 companies like the FDA, Tyson Foods, Boeing, and Hyundai, I can tell you that mental training delivers exponential results. *Magna Mindset* is your edge to outpace competitors and live a life of purpose and success. Your future self will thank you.

Al Batinga
President, Digitized Learning

PREFACE

In 1996, I was named National Rookie of the Year. This achievement was due to my innovative approach to marketing in the insurance industry. When I was hired, the company provided basic marketing tools such as cold-calling leads and magnetic signs for cars and suggested walk-and-talk in the community. I quickly realized these methods were insufficient for achieving my financial goals. This office had over 30 agents, and nationally, there were more than 10,000. I was surrounded by what I can only describe as "mass mediocrity and sheep mentality," a culture of complacency and conformity I wasn't willing to accept.

In the corner of the office, I noticed an 18" by 24" corrugated sign bearing the agency's name. When I asked about it, the manager explained that they give out 3 to 5 of these signs to their agents monthly. Agents can place them in their or neighbors' yards if permitted. However, the manager mentioned that the signs were ineffective and recommended that I stick to the standard marketing tools he had introduced.

PREFACE

The next day, I designed an insurance sign that read, "Affordable Health & Life Insurance," which included three different rates and my toll-free number in large, bold lettering. My first order was for 300 signs; later that year, I ordered 1,000. I went to Home Depot and purchased a 15-foot folding ladder. For the first three weeks, I drove around, nailing signs to telephone poles and staking them at busy intersections throughout Portland and at every major exit off the freeway, overpass, and in various local cities. I continued hanging signs until my pager generated 15 to 20 hot leads daily. Eventually, I became so busy that I no longer had the time to hang signs as I once had.

This approach enabled me to afford direct mailers the following year, starting with one county and eventually expanding to all the counties in Oregon. From that day forward, I engaged in direct mass marketing. After winning a national award, 10,000 other agents nationwide adopted the same sign campaign, significantly increasing the company's national sales production. Throughout my career, I have ranked in the top 1% of the industry for 25 out of 27 years with six different insurance companies.

In the two years I did not achieve this level, I served as the National Insurance Trainer for the top Independent Marketing Organization in the country.

Life is rarely straightforward; in most cases, you are presented with imperfect conditions, and people often give up. You must adjust to the circumstances you find yourself in and invent your future if necessary. Nothing will stand in your way if you have the right mindset to produce the desired results. For the most part, the masses of people in your industry are not your competitors. Your competitor is you! How you think and operate, moving out of your way to allow success to happen. If you're already an elite producer, this book will sharpen your strengths, but it's true purpose is to uplift those

PREFACE

trapped in mediocrity, offering them the tools to rise above and thrive.

Having retired, I have compiled this book as a comprehensive reflection of my journey and training experiences accumulated over the years. A degree is often seen as the benchmark for credibility and expertise in many professions. However, in the field of sales psychology, there is no formal degree to pursue. Instead, true mastery can only be achieved through hands-on experiences and real-world interactions. This book aims to share the invaluable lessons and insights I've gained through a lifetime of engaging with the nuances of human behavior in the context of sales.

> *"We have about 5 choices in our life, we can be bad at what we do, we can be average at what we do, we can be good at what we do, or we can be excellent, or we can be elite. And everybody has a choice as to what they do and how they want to do that.*
>
> *But if you're going to be excellent or elite, you have to do special things, you have to have special intensity, you have to have special focus, you have to have special commitment and drive and passion, to do things at a high level and high standard all the time.*
>
> *It doesn't matter what God-given ability that you have, that will probably make you good, but without the rest of it, I'm not sure you ever get excellent or elite."* - Nick Sabin

WHAT THIS BOOK IS ABOUT

This book is a practical, step-by-step guide to growing a World-Class Mindset in sales and life. Developing elite skills is a by-product of creating a healthy, abundant life. Elite performers possess specific qualities and habits that produce high-performance results. They excel by implementing fundamentals we all share but perform them at a world-class level. This book is a transformative journey of personal growth and development. It starts by identifying your mindset's weaknesses and then guides you in replacing those habits with a mindset that not only excels but will elevate your sales performance.

As you progress through the chapters, you will experience the power to reshape fundamental character traits of behavior, thinking, attitude, belief, work ethic, and sales habits. It will instill in you a deep-seated knowledge and understanding of the mindset of World-Class Producers. This transformation is the key to unlocking the power that leads to exceptional results.

An elite mindset is characterized by specific traits such as resilience, adaptability, and a growth-oriented perspective. Individuals with an elite mindset have learned to overcome their limitations, allowing their full potential to emerge. This book focuses on producing that mindset.

What is a World-Class Mindset

A World-Class Mindset breaks free from the constraints of mediocrity by taking control of life's chessboard, making every move with intention and purpose.

> *A World-Class Mindset is based on the principles of a growth mindset, discipline, and mental toughness. It shapes how you face challenges, view yourself and your circumstances, and take decisive action to drive change. With this mindset, you harness high emotional intelligence, mental flexibility, and self-awareness, enabling you to adapt to new situations and remain open-minded. You possess a sharp awareness of others' emotions and can interpret what they are expressing. You project confidence while staying grounded in humility and consistency. Your constructive mindset allows you to strengthen your character through setbacks. You refuse to let circumstances or others dictate your actions. You recognize that accepting responsibility empowers you to take control of your life. And you will never forget your best friend, "NOW!"*

This book will emphasize the importance of developing your emotional mindset over technical skills. Selling is composed of 80% self-empowerment, relationship building and 20% product knowledge. Elite performers excel at being authentic with others, understanding the psychology behind people's buying decisions, and effectively combining the technical aspects of selling with the emotional needs of clients.

WHAT THIS BOOK IS ABOUT

This combination of psychological fortitude and selling expertise is essential for achieving excellence and breaking through barriers in performance.

While there are countless ways to present yourself and your product, only a few approaches can elevate your abilities to an elite level. Understanding the psychology of selling is like having a secret weapon in your arsenal, granting you the power to influence and persuade effectively with the balance of respect and integrity.

Your active participation in this journey is not just important; it is essential for taking control and shaping your path toward success.

I encourage you to complete all the chapters in order from beginning to end. Each chapter is designed to enhance the next step in developing a powerful mindset.

In summary, your mindset plays a pivotal role in determining your success or failure in sales. It's important to understand that no one is inherently born with a World-Class Mindset; it is a skill that takes time, dedication, and intentional practice to develop.

The key difference lies in getting serious about your goals, letting go of a mindset that denies your potential, and embracing a reality grounded in principles that will help you develop your optimal mental and emotional abilities.

PERFORMANCE GOALS AND OBJECTIVES

1. Differences Between Growth and Fixed Mindset
2. Define the Mindset You Operate From
3. Identify Your Strengths and Weaknesses
4. Evaluate Emotional, Mental, & Technical Blind Spots
5. Understand Sales Psychology
6. Develop Internal and External Self-Awareness
7. Explore the Mindset of World-Class Producers
8. Enhance Emotional Intelligence in Sales
9. Maintain a World-Class Attitude
10. Cultivate World-Class Communication Skills
11. Foster World-Class Mental Toughness
12. Embrace World-Class Responsibility
13. Master Elite Sales Skills
14. Sustain a World-Class Mindset in Sales
15. Understand Emotions That Hinder Success
16. Transform Your Mindset

CHAPTER 1
EVALUATE YOUR MINDSET
WHAT MENTAL OPERATING SYSTEM RUNS YOUR PERFORMANCE?

Most people treat emotions like interruptions. But what if they're instructions? Your beliefs built this ecosystem. Your mindset maintains it. And now it's time to evaluate it.

I will start by asking you a few questions. Have you ever considered why you think the way you do? Can you identify the emotions that drive your mindset? Do you know where your thinking originates? Consider your judgments, thoughts, decision-making processes, and how you determine your self-worth. Your mindset doesn't evolve overnight; it is a product of your past and present experiences and the environment in which you grew up. Let's explore how you answer these questions.

This chapter will examine the origins of your thinking and how it shapes your perception. Your emotions and beliefs contribute to developing your thought processes, shaped by your experiences up to this point. A study conducted by UC Berkeley involving 2,000 participants found that humans experience 27 different emotions, challenging the previous notion held by science and behavioral psychology that there are only six basic emotions. While you have a physical body, you navigate life through a complex body of emotions. We feel the way we do because we think the way we do.

Your emotions and beliefs can be a powerful engine that drives your actions, efforts, and daily decisions, fueling your success. Conversely, if you unconsciously operate from an unproductive mindset, you're dragging a flat tire through life, never understanding why others excel while you struggle. Your emotions and beliefs are not passive; they will empower your success or contribute to your failure. If your mindset imprisons you and continues to believe that you are incapable or that false truths define you, you are a slave to your thinking.

What you think and believe shapes the person you become. These emotions and beliefs are the turbines underneath your ship, guiding your strengths and weaknesses and influencing your efforts, decisions, and challenges. Furthermore, those who underperform and feel stuck often do so from a victim's mindset. They struggle with accountability and may resort to manipulation, control, or blaming others for their mistakes.

Your Perceptions Attract a Frequency

The power of your mindset stems directly from the perceptions, emotions, beliefs, and values you hold. To understand perception better, recognize that it is your unique interpretation of the world around you. Your perception shapes your reality; we don't see the objective reality, but rather our own version of it. Each individual lives within their own perception, and there is no inherent advantage to any one perspective.

Perceptions are accompanied by emotions. These emotions are frequencies we all share, love is one frequency, anger or hate represents another, while pride and confidence form yet another frequency, and feelings of unworthiness exist as well. Every thought you have also carries a frequency. If you lack self-identity and belief in yourself, you may find that you relinquish your power. This is evident in how self-identity and self-perception relate to certain frequencies.

As a result, you are continuously interacting with a quantum field of possibilities and probabilities, within the band of frequency that represents you. You create and attract back into your life the outcomes that align with this frequency. Ultimately, you will live a life that is manifested from your own perception.

What Mindset & Perception Do You Operate From

As you reflect on each concept, ask yourself: Does this way of thinking and perceiving limit my power, or can I thrive while operating from this mindset?

Fixed Mindset: A fixed mindset convinces me that I cannot improve beyond my current state. I feel incapable; if I win, that's great, but if I don't, it doesn't matter to me. I never win at anything, so I don't see the need to change and refuse to do so. Whatever happens, happens. This fixed mindset denies the importance of flexibility, growth, and the effort required to succeed in life and sales.

Weak Mindset: I believe I cannot change my circumstances. My problems and challenges feel more powerful than I am. I often feel lost in life and prefer the easier path, choosing to give up when things get tough. A weak mindset struggles to stick to its goals, lacks a larger purpose, and avoids taking responsibility. People with this mindset often seek validation through friendliness and peer acceptance, opting for the easiest routes. Unfortunately, this approach is neither respected nor trusted by others.

Strong Mindset: This mindset is unyielding in its beliefs, whether right or wrong. It dismisses the possibility of alternative viewpoints and embodies a know-it-all attitude. This mindset is driven by pride and a desire for control. People often find it challenging to engage with it, as it tends to dominate discussions, rarely compromises, and makes connections difficult.

Victim's Mindset: This mindset involves blaming others for the problems in one's life and the difficulties in moving forward. Individuals with this mindset often think, "If only others would be kind and help me, I might have a chance." They may attribute their struggles to their parents or believe that other people are the reason they can't succeed. This perspective often employs martyrdom to feel persecuted, gain attention, and avoid responsibility. Such individuals are convinced that life is not only out of their control but is also intentionally trying to harm them.

Passive Mindset: This mindset operates under the belief that things will work out on their own. It assumes that life unfolds regardless of any real effort on the individual's part. People with this mindset often wait for their "ship to come in." They live in a state of denial, never taking enough initiative or having a productive plan. They frequently ask themselves why bad things happen to them and seek ways to avoid taking responsibility.

Negative Mindset: This mindset is characterized by self-doubt, pessimism, and fear, which can manifest both consciously and unconsciously. Individuals may think, "I can never do anything right," or "I wonder if I will ever get a sale." They may feel that "it's not worth it" or believe that even if they succeed, they will fail again. This state of constant worry is destructive and self-sabotaging, blocking success and preventing individuals from taking action and achieving their goals.

Prideful Mindset: This mindset involves an inability to accept constructive criticism and is characterized by arrogance and disdain. An inflated sense of accomplishment and success fuels it. Those with a prideful mindset often speak grandly but fail to back it up with actions. They falsely believe in their importance and greatness, usually summarized by the phrase, "Big hat, no cattle." People with this mindset struggle to accept their failures and are typically defensive when scrutinizing their behavior. While they may hold considerable power, it is often based on pretense. Their underlying insecurities and fears drive this mindset, including concerns about humility, vulnerability, and low self-esteem. They impose impossible perfection standards on themselves, further fueling their pride.

Growth Mindset: A growth mindset embraces change and views challenges as opportunities for learning and improvement. It expresses enthusiasm for personal growth with statements like, "I am excited to change! I can change, and I am ready to learn whatever is necessary to improve my situation with myself and others. I can be better." This attitude is adaptable, recognizing that change is a part of life. It welcomes constructive criticism and understands that failure is a valuable lesson in success. Individuals with a growth mindset are humble and emotionally intelligent; they accept responsibility for their actions, are self-aware, and can admit when they are wrong. They are sensitive to the feelings of others and understand the importance of being mentally flexible, which are foundational strengths of this mindset.

Your Mindset Is the Holy Grail of How You Operate

The mindset you operate from influences your business, relationships, and financial goals. Depending on circumstances, people often have various perspectives and may draw from more than one mindset. A person with a fixed mindset might exhibit a weak mindset, succumbing to challenges and setbacks, or a strong mindset that prevents them from considering alternative approaches. This can lead to feelings of hopelessness and a reluctance to try again. Over time, this mindset can shift into a victim mentality.

We have discussed various mindsets, including weak, strong, victim, passive, negative, and prideful mindsets, among others not mentioned. It's important to understand that all these mindsets fall under the umbrella of a fixed mindset because they can limit your emotional potential and hinder your ability to succeed.

The Quality of Your Thinking Will Determine the Quality of Your Life

Approximately 70-80% of salespeople struggle to make a living or quit in 1-3 years. Why are only a select few consistently top producers? The answer lies in your perspective; your emotional and mental makeup is crucial in determining your success or failure in professional sales and life. It's important to ask yourself: Do I have a fixed mindset? How much of my thinking is influenced by that fixed mindset? In her book, *Mindset: The New Psychology of Success*, author Carol Dweck, Ph.D., brings to light her extensive research over the past 30 years, concluding that people generally adopt one of two mindsets: a "Fixed Mindset" or a "Growth Mindset." She explains that this development begins in childhood.

> *"The fixed mindset limits your abilities and reinforces a sense of failure, while the growth mindset eliminates self-doubt and views opportunities and experiences as part of personal growth. Most people who struggle in business and seek help to reach their goals tend to operate from a fixed mindset. With a fixed mindset, you form predetermined ideas about yourself and your abilities, setting yourself up for failure even before*

you begin. As a result, you can only perform at a predetermined level of expectation. This is why many individuals underperform, give up, or quit. Once this destructive mindset takes hold, it perpetuates a cycle of failure. Your mind dictates what you can or cannot achieve, leaving no room for improvement or advancement."

How do you recognize when you are operating from a fixed mindset? Your mind acts like a powerful programming system; past experiences and emotions influence your self-perception and abilities. Many of your actions and decision-making processes stem from your history, such as your upbringing, school experiences, bullying, lacking friendships, facing failures in front of others, feeling embarrassed, encountering tragedy, developing a sense of entitlement, and avoiding personal responsibility. All these experiences and emotions have shaped and constrained your understanding of who you are today. By recognizing this, you can become more self-aware and intentionally shift your mindset.

Start by acknowledging this type of thinking when it surfaces. No matter how intelligent or skilled you may be, these mindsets can deplete your coping resources, which are the mental and emotional tools you use to deal with challenges. It's also crucial to realize that when you're not confronting failure, stress, or demanding circumstances, individuals with a fixed mindset are just as deserving and hopeful as those with a growth mindset.

Your mindset is the holy grail of how you operate, positively or negatively influencing every aspect of your life. If you remain stuck in a limiting mindset and fail to recognize what's holding you back, it can significantly impact your ability to achieve your goals. Those who succeed quickly and easily in sales tend to adopt a growth mindset. Operating outside of this mindset restricts your emotional strength and potential for growth. You are not accountable for the conditioning you received in childhood; however, as an adult, you are fully responsible for addressing it. When you choose to operate from a mindset that denies your potential, you forfeit your ability to change. Remember, you possess the power to transform your situation. This book will assist you in developing healthy beliefs and emotional habits and staying grounded in your strengths. However, transforming your life comes with a cost: stepping out of your comfort zone. Many people are not truly stuck; they are simply afraid of change. Embracing change requires confronting discomfort to some extent. It represents the journey toward becoming the person you aspire to be. The objective of change is not to return to an ideal situation in your life but to cultivate the ability to navigate imperfect conditions with the potential for significant growth.

"The measure of intelligence is the ability to change" - Albert Einstein

Dr. Bruce Lipton talk- Author of Biology of Belief Conscious Mind in Formative Years – Excerpt

"Right behind your forehead lies the prefrontal cortex, the seat of your conscious mind. This part of your brain is where your wishes, desires, and aspirations reside. It's where you envision your life and get creative. This is the part of your mind that empowers you to shape your future.

The conscious mind is about 10%, and the rest of the brain, 90%, is called the subconscious mind. The subconscious mind is primarily a habit; the fundamental habits did not come from me. During the last tri-meister of pregnancy and the first seven years of life, your brain is operating at a low vibrational frequency called theta, which is hypnosis.

How do you learn to be a member of a family and a community and culture? You watch other people; you focus on your family, see how they do everything, and learn from everybody else. So, the programs that you get from the first 7 years are not yours, they came from other people, and they passed that on to you, but the problem is it's not just the previous generation, the generation before, and the generation before, etc.

So, we passed it down through the family. Here is the problem —big time! Science has found that 95% of our lives are spent thinking. When the conscious mind is thinking, it's not paying attention. The subconscious program is the default when the conscious mind is not paying attention.

Well, if you understand that, then it's only 5% of the time, you are running your life with your creative mind, wishes and desires, and what you want. 95% of your life comes from the program. Yeah, but the program is not your wishes and desires; it's other people's behavior, 95% of the day you are playing programs that psychologists tell us are limiting, disempowering, self-sabotaging, all of us, every one of us every day plays programs that we don't see and there not ours, all we see is the result, and we say, this is not what I wanted, yes, but this is what you created."

Your perception of yourself was shaped long before you became an adult. It's important to understand that your past experiences, such as being praised for your academic achievements or facing frequent criticism, have a significant impact on how you view yourself. Your attitudes and self-esteem were ingrained in you during your formative years. Everything you experience today goes through this lens. In many ways, you are a culmination of your past experiences, living in the present.

It's not uncommon for people to carry the weight of their emotional baggage, guilt, and low self-esteem, which can sabotage their potential. However, by engaging in self-reflection, you can begin to understand the roots of these feelings and take steps to overcome them. When these feelings resurface under stress or in high-pressure situations that require performance, you can use your self-awareness to see things differently and break free from the trap of your mindset.

Remember, your subconscious mind is not set in stone. It constantly reminds you of past experiences but is also open to change. You can reprogram it to respond differently when faced with opportunities, risks, or challenges. Your mind can tell you, "I can do that; I can succeed; I will try and learn from any outcome." This shift in mindset is the key to unlocking your potential and living a more fulfilling life. You have the power to shape your self-perception and mindset.

It is possible to break free from this fixed thinking. By actively practicing self-awareness, courageously and consistently challenging negative thoughts, and eagerly seeking new experiences, you can begin to see things from a different perspective. Your journey to personal growth starts with these proactive steps.

The Power of a Growth Mindset

Let's discuss the power of a growth mindset, starting with a few questions. What are the key factors for success in any vocation? What distinguishes two individuals with the same tools and disposition, yet one excels while the other struggles in mediocrity? Is it personality, intelligence, demeanor, or work ethic? Or could it be that one possesses a mindset free from predetermined limits?

Research shows that the most empowering asset is the ability to step outside one's comfort zone, trust the unknown, and take action regardless of uncertainty. Individuals enhance their potential and build emotional resilience by learning to move forward without a guarantee of success.

No judgments, fear, or "what-ifs"—none of those matters. You have what it takes to achieve your goal: one sale daily and 50 calls a week. You are committed to managing your time effectively to reach this objective. This is the hallmark of a growth mindset.

A growth mindset allows you to thrive during challenging times. Those with this mindset view failure as an opportunity for growth, embracing trials and challenges. They do not label or judge themselves, nor do they give up. Instead, they confront setbacks directly and find ways to succeed. At the core of this mindset is the belief in change. When things don't go as planned, or you need to improvise, you push through to complete the task. You go above and beyond what is expected to get the job done.

Setbacks can paralyze individuals with a fixed mindset. They are often unwilling to step outside their comfort zones. When faced with difficulties, they may feel powerless and incapable, making it hard to take even the most straightforward actions to improve their situation. When something begins to slip away, they still feel helpless.

In contrast, individuals with a growth mindset confront challenges head-on and embrace the reality of difficult situations. They are willing to stretch themselves when necessary, demonstrating courage and resilience in the face of adversity.

However, everyone tends to rely on the mindset that feels most comfortable to them. Rarely do individuals operate with a wholly fixed or altogether growth mindset; instead, we often embody a mix of both. Those who consistently succeed in overcoming challenges and achieving their goals tend to exhibit optimism, mental flexibility, and the ability to adapt to new situations. They are more willing to embrace a growth mindset.

Individuals who struggle in business, relationships, and life often operate primarily from a fixed mindset. It may come as a surprise, but success in sales is not solely driven by talent or skill. What truly distinguishes elite producers is the strength and adaptability of their mindset.

Mental flexibility is all about adaptability. A healthy mindset's core is the ability to adjust to new situations and switch between different mental tasks. This includes effectively navigating changes in your environment, being aware of yourself and others, and self-regulating your emotions. Elite performers often demonstrate remarkably flexible personalities, showcasing their adaptability and open-mindedness.

When self-aware and equipped with high emotional and mental skills, facing challenges feels as effortless as a knife cutting through soft butter. This self-awareness is key for confronting adversity with emotional strength. Such a mindset empowers you in every presentation, call, and complicated situation.

Having a growth mindset is like having powerful turbines propelling your ship through life and in sales. This shift in thinking can produce valuable skills and outcomes, leading to habits rooted in excellence, perseverance, commitment, intensity, drive, passion, and focus. When you begin to move out of your way, you begin to magnify your strengths.

These are the qualities of a World-Class Mindset. Nothing can overshadow these strengths, which distinguish elite producers from the average. However, it's essential to recognize that no one is perfect. Setbacks are inevitable; you may occasionally fall back into old thought patterns. Stay present and be aware when this happens!

Begin to Change Beliefs, Values and Mindset

The truth is you have the power to create whatever you desire. However, the most significant barrier between where you are now and where you want to be is yourself, not time, money, or circumstances. You are your greatest obstacle. Your competition comes from bad habits, distractions, insecurities, fear, low self-confidence, belief in yourself, pride, procrastination, and a lack of discipline.

As Marcus Aurelius, the Emperor of Rome, wisely stated, "We can't control what happens to us in life, but we can control how we respond to what happens." It's not the events themselves that matter, but rather your reaction to those events.

Neuroscience and Your Mind
Dr. Joe Dispenza –Best Selling Author Expert on Neuroscience and Quantum Physics

"We may not be able to control everything in our outer world, but we can control our inner world; it's not important that you react; everybody reacts; the question is how long will you react. If you keep an emotional reaction going on for an extended period, you are memorizing that emotion and your body, as the unconscious mind believes. Neuroscience has found that the body doesn't know the difference between the real experience producing emotion and the emotion we create by thought alone. When you are living by some emotion, there will always be a gap between how things appear and how things really are - emotions alter our perceptions."

Our thoughts shape and define our reality. When we focus on problems, we tend to attract more problems. Conversely, when we concentrate on solutions, we uncover more opportunities. By dwelling on the negative, we inadvertently reinforce those aspects in our minds. Our mental habits play a significant role in shaping our identity. Our brains function like supercomputers that follow the instructions we provide, and they are inclined to believe the narratives we repeatedly tell ourselves.

Begin to Train Your Mind
Dr. Richard Louismiller – Clinical Psychologist

"The mind listens to everything that is going around it, and it also listens to everything that's going on inside of it. That means that if you criticize yourself or say negative things about yourself, not only does the mind record it, but it affects your well-being and your emotional state; this is the same if you say positive things about yourself. If you say positive things about yourself, called affirmations, and you do it regularly, your mind starts to believe it and soak it in, and it becomes a part of you. Begin to train yourself to be aware of what you are thinking. One of the ways to do that is to periodically say to yourself, what am I thinking? Would I like this thought to create my life? Would I want to have the experience this thought could bring me?"

What you repeatedly say to yourself truly matters! Hebb's law, which examines the relationship between psychology and neuroscience, states that behavior originates in the brain and is based on neural networks or patterns. This principle emphasizes that your self-talk shapes your brain, influencing your beliefs, driving your behavior, and creating your thoughts, feelings, and experiences. Ultimately, this forms the perspective of your reality. What you affirm to yourself most frequently will become your reality!

Beliefs are what you consider to be true, while values represent what you deem essential. Changing your mindset can be challenging when your reality is deeply rooted in your beliefs, as they influence your sense of self, ego, self-esteem, and self-worth. These factors shape how you perceive yourself and your potential.

When you begin to see yourself as a person who values curiosity and embraces change, you allow your experiences to shape your growth. By concentrating on the positive aspects of life and letting go of the negative, you develop a mindset focused on learning and continual improvement. Establishing healthy habits supports this transformation.

Habits Shape Our Identity

Healthy habits attract and drive success. Success is not something you pursue; it is something you attract through your thoughts and actions. You become successful by developing positive habits that shape your personality, work, relationships, and self-perception. Your thoughts and choices play a key role in this process.

So, how can you cultivate these habits? First, recognize that habits shape your identity. Take a moment to assess your current habits and their impact on your performance and success. What are you doing each day? Consider which habits contribute to your success and which hold you back. Reflect on your daily routines, starting from the moment you wake up. When we dwell on the past or fixate on the future, we create negative habits that weaken our power and character. Practicing mindfulness and focusing on the present moment allows your emotions to engage fully with your current experience. You feel alive and excited, free from the burdens of unresolved issues. By staying present, you can effectively address whatever challenges arise, whether they are good or bad.

It is important to recognize that the best way to influence the past and future is by focusing on the present. Our present actions continuously shape both our past and our future. If you fail to ground yourself in the "NOW", you inadvertently create the very outcomes you want to avoid. Negative memories, future worries, and unproductive habits stem from actions or inactions in the present. Unhealthy habits can hinder your potential to grow and thrive each day.

These negative behaviors contribute to distractions, procrastination, insecurities, fear, a lack of discipline, and the belief in false truths about yourself. These emotions and choices can weaken your mental strength and keep you outside your power zone, which consists of intention, action, practice, consistency, and discipline. To create positive change, start with a clear purpose. Take daily action, remain consistent, and allow these actions to become habits over time.

This process will shape who you are. Your habits define you; what you do today reflects who you will be tomorrow. Remember, you don't attract what you want; you attract who you are. By striving to become the best version of yourself, you will naturally manifest what you desire.

> *"People do not decide their futures. They decide their habits, and their habits decide their futures."* - Fredrick M. Alexander

Change Your Energy Change Your Life
Dr. Joe Dispenza - Author and Speaker

"Your personality creates your reality. If you want to change your reality and life, you must change your personality. You need to start thinking about what you have been thinking about and change it. You must become conscious of your unconscious habits and behaviors and modify them. And

then, you need to look at certain emotions that keep you anchored to the past. And ask the most critical question. Do these emotions belong in my future? The problem with these survival emotions is that they are like a narcotic; they're like a drug. They give the brain and body a rush of energy, and people, over time, become addicted to the very rush of those survival chemicals. They use the people and the problems in their life and their past to reaffirm their addiction to that emotion, which means they need the bad job, they need the poor relationship, they need the bad memories because it makes them feel something. So then, "even though it's not a good feeling." This means they become addicted to the life they don't even like. And this is why change is so hard. So then, just like an addict overcoming a drug, when people start to change, they must go through these periods where they are in withdrawal.

The next question is, what thought do you want to fire and wire in your brain? Close your eyes and begin to review those thoughts; what behaviors do you want to change or demonstrate? The latest neuroscience research says that in the act of closing your eyes and rehearsing your behaviors, you begin to change your brain to look like that experience has already happened. "The science of mental rehearsal says you can change your brain to look like you already did it. The practice of rehearsing how you will be in certain circumstances, you install more neurological hardware, the brain does not know the difference between the real-life experience and what you are imagining. Teaching your body emotionally what it feels like before the experience takes time; you live in the feeling as often as you can to condition your body."

In other words, you are installing the neurological hardware in your brain, and if you keep doing it repeatedly, the hard-

ware becomes a software program; what does that mean? You start acting like a happy person. Why? There is no magic there; you installed the circuits. You start thinking in more unlimited ways because you put those in place.

Now, here's the tough part. Can you teach your body emotionally what that future will feel like before that's made manifest? That means you can't wait for healing to feel gratitude and wholeness; you can't wait for your wealth to feel abundance and worthiness; you can't wait for the mystical moment to feel awe; that's the old model of reality of cause and effect, it's Newtonian physics. But the new model of reality, the quantum model of reality, is about causing effect, which means the moment you start feeling gratitude and whole, your healing begins. The moment you start feeling worthy, you are generating wealth.

The moment you are in awe of life, you will have a mystical experience, so then your body is your unconscious mind. It does not know the difference between an actual experience in your life that creates an emotion and an emotion you can create by thought alone, so the body is believing it's living in that future reality in the present moment.

What is significant about that, as I said, is that the latest research in genetics says genes don't create disease; the environment signals the gene that creates change. Well, the end product of experience and the environment is an emotion. The moment you embrace an elevated emotion, you are signaling the gene ahead of the environment and what genes do; genes make proteins, and what are proteins responsible for, the structure and function of your body, and the expression of proteins is the expression of life. If you keep knocking on that genetic door over and over again, you are going to begin to up-regulate the genes for health. You're going to down-regulate the genes for disease, and suddenly, you are going to wake up in your dream; you are a different person."

You see the thoughts you think are the electrical charge in the quantum field. The feeling you emote is the magnetic charge in the quantum field. How you think and how you feel are broadcasts and electromagnetic signatures that influence every single atom in your life. The thought sends the signal out, and the feeling draws the event back. So, if you are walking around your life feeling sorry for yourself like a victim. You are broadcasting that signature into the field. And you will create more experiences to suffer because we are not punished for our sins; we are punished by our sins. And sin is an attitude, and sin is how you think and feel.

So, when you cause people to give up their guilt, shame, and unworthiness and teach them how to open their hearts and create coherent waves in their brains and hearts, they're going to produce the miraculous. It takes training, practice, learning new information, and deprogramming ourselves into believing that we are limited.

But if you're living by the hormones of stress and you have no energy, no field. Then you can't produce an effect on matter. So then, life is about managing energy, and where you place your attention is where you put your energy. And suppose your intention is on knowns and the predictable future, or your attention is on the familiar emotions of the past. In that case, you are siphoning energy out of the present moment and have no energy to create with. And when you can do this and practice it well, you will begin to do what's innately your birthright, and that is to create an unknown or wonderful experience in your life."

"If you want to find the secrets of the universe, think in terms of energy, frequency and vibration."

- Nikola Tesla

6 Rules of Changing Your Energy and Frequency

Understanding that everything in the universe operates at a certain frequency, including our thoughts and emotions, can help us better manage our energy and mindset.

1. Start each day with gratitude. Acknowledge and appreciate the good things in your life. Gratitude breeds a positive attitude, peace, and acceptance.
2. For the first 20 minutes of the morning, practice self-affirmation, which involves consciously repeating positive statements about yourself. Train your brain to think of these positive affirmations. This will reinforce a positive self-image and boost your confidence.
3. Visualize and feel what you desire to attract in your life. Act daily, stay consistent, and develop positive habits over time; this will shape who you are.
4. Problems are opportunities to exercise and maintain an attitude of resilience. Problems are a part of life and it's not necessary to label them as negative. Stay positive when you are under stress or challenged, practice focusing on the solution rather than stuck on the problem.
5. Healthy habits attract and drive success. Success is not something you pursue; it is something you attract through your thoughts and actions. Develop positive habits that shape your personality, work, relationships, and self-perception.

6. **Celebrate small wins.** Recognizing and celebrating even the smallest of achievements allows you to feel accomplished and positive, boosting your morale and self-esteem.

Open a New Room You Have Never Entered

As we conclude this chapter, embrace the opportunity to transcend your old thinking and remain open to the possibilities of a new you. Close your eyes and imagine opening the door to a room you have never entered before. In this space, you are free to build a new mindset. Visualize yourself stepping into this room. There is nothing inside; it is entirely new. Your old self and way of thinking cannot enter this space.

From this moment forward, as we continue through this book, you will learn, grow, and evolve in this room, distinct from your old mindset. Give this room a name you can call on, e.g. "I now live, think and act from my Power Room". This room now serves as the foundation for a **Growth Mindset**. Stay in this room and think from this perspective as we work together to expand the values and principles of a World-Class Mindset.

Fixed Mindset Questionnaire

Instructions:

Rate your agreement with each statement below using the following scale: Be honest—this is about self-awareness, not perfection.

1 = Never (0% of the time)
2 = Rarely (less than 25%)
3 = Sometimes (about 50%)
4 = Often (about 75%)
5 = Always (100%)

Section 1: Self-Worth and Intelligence

1.	I feel pressure to prove I'm intelligent in conversations.	
2.	I often feel anxious about saying something foolish.	
3.	I worry my abilities aren't obvious, so I try hard to show competence.	
4.	I need to earn others' respect by appearing capable.	
5.	I measure my worth by how competent I seem.	
6.	I worry that mistakes make me look unintelligent.	
7.	If I don't perform well, I question my abilities.	

Section 2: Identity and Fixed Traits

8.	I believe people are either talented or not, there's not much in between.	
9.	I tend to see challenges as tests of who I am.	
10.	My traits seem permanent; I struggle to change them easily.	
11.	Failure feels like a reflection of my character.	
12.	I believe intelligence is a fixed trait.	

Section 3: External Validation and Comparison

13.	I often compare myself to others and feel behind.	
14.	I worry about what others think of me nearly all the time.	
15.	I feel the need to prove myself repeatedly.	
16.	I struggle to feel good enough without others' approval.	
17.	I find it hard to stay motivated if I don't feel successful.	

Section 4: Struggle, Control, and Growth Resistance

18.	I hesitate to try difficult things; I might fail.	
19.	When things get hard, I tend to give up.	
20.	I feel stuck in areas of my life, even when I try.	
21.	I feel more secure when I'm in total control.	
22.	I believe success depends more on luck or circumstances than effort.	

Scoring: (Total Possible Score: 22 - 110)

Add up your total score	

Score 22–44 / Growth-Oriented - *You strongly embody a growth mindset. Setbacks rarely define you; you lean into effort. You generally believe in your capacity to grow and adapt. Mistakes are seen as learning opportunities, not identity threats. You're more likely to take constructive risks, persist through difficulties, and remain open to feedback. When setbacks happen, you may feel discomfort, but you reflect and recalibrate rather than crumble. There's a foundation of self-compassion and a focus on process over perfection.*

Score 45–66 / Mixed Tendencies - *You show a healthy mix of growth and fixed mindset tendencies. You lean toward growth mindset behaviors but still experience moments of self-doubt or ego-*

driven comparison. You may feel pressure to prove yourself in unfamiliar or high stakes situations and occasionally avoid challenges for fear of failure. These tendencies don't dominate, but they can quietly drain energy and limit risk-taking. With awareness and intentional mindset work, you're well-positioned to strengthen flexibility and self-belief.

Score 67–88 / Fixed Leaning - *A stronger influence of fixed beliefs shows up here. You may avoid certain challenges, downplay effort, or ruminate when things go wrong. Criticism can feel personal, and self-worth may be tied closely to being seen as "smart," "capable," or "likable." You might frequently compare yourself to others or feel paralyzed by setbacks. These patterns aren't permanent but left unchecked, they can limit resilience and stunt personal development.*

Score 89–110 / Strong Fixed Mindset - *Your thinking may be heavily shaped by fear of failure, deep sensitivity to perceived judgment, and a belief that your traits or situation are largely unchangeable. You may struggle to re-engage after setbacks, internalize challenges as personal flaws, or feel chronically stuck or inadequate. The need to prove yourself or hide perceived weaknesses might override curiosity or growth. This score isn't a label it's a flag that you're in a mindset loop that can be rewritten with courage, support, and purposeful reflection.*

MAGNA MINDSET

Growth Mindset Questionnaire

Instructions:

Rate your agreement with each statement below using the following scale: Be honest—this is about self-awareness, not perfection.

1 = Always (100%)
2 = Often (about 75%)
3 = Sometimes (about 50%)
4 = Rarely (less than 25%)
5 = Never (0% of the time)

Section 1: Beliefs About Ability

1.	I believe intelligence isn't fixed and can grow with learning.	
2.	Talent can be cultivated, not just inherited.	
3.	I feel confident I can improve if I put in consistent effort.	
4.	I believe challenges help shape and grow my abilities.	
5.	I think learning is a continuous process, not a destination.	
6.	Improvement is possible in subjects I'm not good at.	

Section 2: Response to Setbacks

7.	I bounce back from failure instead of giving up.	
8.	I ask for help or feedback when something doesn't go well.	
9.	I analyze what went wrong and adjust my approach.	
10.	I stay engaged even when progress is slow or invisible.	
11.	I try new strategies when the current ones aren't working.	
12.	I view obstacles as a sign that I'm learning something new.	

Section 3: Approach to Effort and Learning

13.	I embrace hard work as part of the process of growth.	
14.	I stay curious even when the answer isn't immediately clear.	
15.	I enjoy learning more than simply performing well.	
16.	I continue practicing even when it feels frustrating.	
17.	I set learning goals that focus on long-term progress.	
18.	I reflect on what I've learned, not just what I've achieved.	

Section 4: Attitude Toward Others' Success

19.	I find motivation in others' achievements rather than discouragement.	
20.	I strive to learn from those who are more experienced than I am.	
21.	I don't let comparisons diminish my self-worth.	
22.	I support others in their growth journeys.	
23.	I believe everyone is capable of growth with effort and time.	
24.	I feel genuinely happy when others succeed.	

Scoring: (Total Possible Score: 24–120)

Add up your total score	

Score 24–48 / Strong Growth Mindset – *You consistently view intelligence, talent, and success as qualities that can be developed. You embrace learning, effort, and resilience. Challenges fuel your development. Setbacks only strengthen your commitment to progress. You celebrate others' wins without self-doubt. You likely embody the mindset of a lifelong learner.*

Score 49–72 / Moderate Growth Mindset – *You're actively building resilience and adaptive strategies. You generally believe in* *personal growth, but there may be specific areas (such as handling failure or staying engaged) where fixed mindset patterns sneak in under stress or uncertainty. Reflect on areas where doubt arises and use them as opportunities to strengthen your mindset.*

Score 73–96 / Mixed Mindset — *You recognize the value of growth, but your views may shift depending on the context. You likely believe in growth for others but may hold back belief in your own capacity at times. Identifying these blocks can help you develop a stronger commitment to self-improvement. Developing greater consistency in your approach to effort, feedback, and setbacks will deepen your growth mindset.*

Score: 97–120 / Fixed Mindset Tendencies — *You may currently see abilities and intelligence as mostly innate or unchangeable. Setbacks may feel like personal limitations rather than opportunities for growth. But the good news is awareness is the first catalyst for change. With intentional reflection and practice, you can shift toward a growth mindset, strengthening your ability to embrace learning and adaptability. By using this insight, you're already laying the foundation for transformation.*

CHAPTER 2
RESISTANCE, FEAR, AND FAILURE
WHERE YOUR GREATEST STRENGTHS LIE WAITING TO BE UNLEASHED

In chapter 1, Evaluate Your Mindset, we discussed the mental and emotional factors that form the foundation of a World-Class Mindset, shifting your thinking from a fixed thinking to embracing change through a growth mindset. As we begin chapter 2, Resistance: Fear and Failure, the subsequent chapters will build upon the fundamentals of a growth mindset. With this mindset, your sales performance has unlimited potential for growth and improvement.

Before breakthroughs, there's always a battlefield. Not outside you but inside. Resistance, fear, and failure aren't enemies. They're indicators. And if you learn to decode them, you'll stop retreating from discomfort and start leveraging it.

Let's take a deeper look into the concept of resistance in sales. What exactly is resistance, in what various forms does it present itself, and how does it influence your mental outlook? Psychological resistance, often manifested through the denial of one's feelings and emotions, is an overwhelming element in sales. Understanding and applying this concept will give you the tools and confidence needed to overcome challenges and succeed in your sales efforts.

Research in psychology reveals that resistance often emerges from deep-seated feelings of anxiety, an overwhelming fear of failure, chronic procrastination, and the absence of a clear, structured plan. If you find yourself caught in the grip of this resistance, you may notice a range of telltale signs. You might find yourself complaining more frequently about your circumstances, wasting precious hours instead of being productive, neglecting essential prospecting efforts, and feeling a pervasive lack of motivation.

This can lead to unmet sales goals as you inadvertently replace valuable sales time with personal activities that divert your focus. If you allow yourself to remain in a state of resistance for too long, you risk impairing your performance and hindering the development of a World-Class Mindset. We are challenged to move forward whenever we introduce resistance in our bodies. This resistance can manifest as negative emotions or self-doubt, creating an invisible wall between who we think we are and who we want to be.

Fear is the most significant barrier people face in sales. It encompasses various anxieties, including the fear of failure, making phone calls, hearing "No," being disliked and confronting the unknown, such as the worry about not meeting production goals.

This list goes on. Fear is a frequency that manifests through our thoughts. It can intensify fixed thinking, distorting our feelings and perceptions. The truth is that things are often better than we perceive. We are never as inadequate as we feel. Fear tends to anticipate failure, which hinders our potential and paralyzes our ability to focus on our strengths. It is perhaps the most well-known "paper tiger" in our lives.

However, it is necessary to face these emotions directly. This bold step requires courage but can transform your inner struggle into a powerful catalyst for change, energizing your journey to overcome resistance and achieve your objectives.

Our mindset becomes stronger when we practice confronting and moving through our fears. We begin to take ownership of these moments and manage our emotions, a needed skill that makes us more resilient and capable. This approach is far more effective than allowing ourselves to be intimidated by any situation, person or challenge. This empowerment is critical for overcoming fear in sales.

Understanding Resistance Fear and Failure

Another form of resistance is failure, which is closely related to fear. However, failure often results from actions rather than thoughts. When you experience failure and choose to define yourself by it rather than viewing it as a constructive lesson, you limit your ability to succeed in sales. Failure can be transformed into strength, a key aspect of a World-Class Mindset.

Michael Jordan is a powerful example of this. He once said, "I have missed over 9,000 shots in my career. I have lost almost 300 games. Twenty-six times, I have been trusted to take the winning shot and missed. I have failed over and over again, and that is why I succeeded!" Jordan's story is a testament to the power of mental strength. His positive attitude, deep-seated belief in himself, and emotional and mental toughness were stronger than his fear of failure. This empowerment and control over fear is what sets successful individuals apart.

In his first year as a professional, his team reached the playoffs, and Koby Bryant was the young superstar. In the last minute of the game, he had three shots to win it for his team but missed all three. At the end of the game, commentators were astounded that such a talented player had failed to make a single shot. He sat on the bench with his head in his hands, and the commentators speculated about how terrible he must feel. When he got up to leave the court, they managed to interview him and asked, "Koby, you sat on the bench with your head in your hands; you must have felt awful." He looked at them and replied, "What does feeling have to do with it? I was figuring out why I missed those shots. Now I know why I missed them and can do something about it."

Koby's perspective on failure was not to dwell on the missed shots, but to analyze the problem and prepare for the next opportunity to play. This is the mindset of champions, who set aside any emotions hindering their performance. Setbacks can throw you off emotionally, but they also present a valuable learning opportunity. You must go beyond those feelings to understand why you experienced the setback, what you can learn from it, how to avoid it in the future, and how to move forward.

Failure is the rubber that meets the road of your character. Character and mental strength are not built by people merely telling you how great you are or by celebrating victories. Instead, character is forged in the painful moments when you must confront the destruction around you, through loss or heartache. Each time you experience this; you encounter a fork in the road. Your response can either deepen your pain and disappointment or strengthen and refine your emotional resilience, a key to your personal growth and empowerment. This doesn't mean you won't feel these emotions; it means you learn to keep moving forward, determined and resilient. You come to realize that you have the capacity to endure, especially when your limits and boundaries are tested. You survive and emerge stronger than before. Resistance, Fear and Failure are not there to stop you; they exist to show you that you care. Don't resist them. Instead, when you befriend and confront them, they lose their power. This experience reveals where your greatest strengths lie, waiting to be unleashed.

This perspective will embolden your success. How you process your emotions can either strengthen your resolve or weaken your ability to persevere. A World-Class Mindset understands that overcoming Resistance, Fear and Failure, is essential on the journey to success and recognizes the benefits that come from this struggle. If you choose the path of self-pity, believing that you are not good enough or that you cannot achieve your goals, those beliefs will become your reality. It's important to understand that self-pity is a hindrance to your achievement, and by recognizing this, you can be motivated to overcome it. Performance is key in both sales and life. How can you maintain a World-Class Mindset if these challenges and emotions continue to weigh you down? The answer is simple: you cannot.

Fear-based emotions can undermine your ability to excel and limit your potential at work. It can hurt you when you believe you are not good enough or feel intimidated by rejection. Instead of viewing rejection as an opportunity for growth, you may fall into a pattern of negative thinking that reinforces a fixed mindset. A fixed mindset focuses on personal problems and seeks excuses for why you cannot perform, often rooted in these emotions. If you allow this mentality to persist, it will continue to hinder your growth. Therefore, it's essential to learn how to manage these emotions effectively.

Managing Resistance, Fear, and Failure

You will dramatically enhance your emotional and mental strength by effectively managing Resistance, Fear, and Failure. As you do this, you'll find excitement in your pursuits, along with newfound energy and enthusiasm, no longer hiding behind denial or false emotions. Your focus will be on yourself, dedicating 100% effort each day and embracing the results.

It's natural to experience rejection, disappointment, and self-doubt, but it's important to remain focused on your goals. Let these emotions flow like water over a rock but never lose sight of your objectives. This determination will guide you through the toughest of times. There's no judgment or labeling if you have a bad call, appointment, or setback, it simply is what it is. Keep moving forward and stay productive.

This approach empowers you to build momentum, as each positive experience lays the groundwork for the next. Over time, negative emotions such as resistance, fear, and failure will carry less weight. As this transformation occurs, you are integrating a World-Class Mindset in your life and sales, feeling patient and understanding of the process.

5 Steps to Manage - Resistance, Fear, and Failure

1. Perception vs Perspective

A World-Class Mindset views resistance, fear, and failure as perceptions rather than burdens. These are choices you can make in how you deal with them. This perspective is changeable. By shifting from perception to perspective, you move your focus away from your worries, doubts and concerns and begin to observe the experiences, thoughts, and feelings of others. In doing so, you open yourself to understanding how to make a difference and acting in the world around you. This shift increases our sense of connection, empathy and confidence. When you take the focus off yourself, you experience less resistance, and your energy can be redirected toward finding solutions, making you more proactive and resourceful.

2. Focus on the Fundamentals

Focus on each action that leads to success: "I need to set three appointments today," "I need to practice my script," "I need to prepare for my next meeting," and "I need to make 50 calls this week to reach my goal." Direct your focus to the process. You can reduce resistance by acting and being proactive. When fear or thoughts of failure arise, address them immediately with purpose rather than letting them grow stronger.

3. How to Process Failure

When life tells you that you are failing, and the facts support that perception, it's easy to dwell on your shortcomings. However, a World-Class Mindset views challenges as opportunities for growth. They don't harshly judge themselves; instead, they ask questions and seek to understand the lessons behind their experiences. They focus on how to apply what they've learned to create positive change. Failing is a natural part of life; the key lies in how you process those failures.

4. Break Through Fear and Failure

Confront your fears and the possibility of failure directly. Whatever your fear may be, make a plan to move through it. It was performing stand-up comedy in the '80s, which was my greatest fear. The experience challenged me in ways I never could have imagined. It was a powerful exercise in managing this challenge, and the benefits have been enormous. Since then, no person, situation, challenge, or intimidation has felt too big for me. This experience took my confidence and trust in myself to a level I might not have reached otherwise. I encourage you to be bold, exercise and test your doubt, push your boundaries further, and begin the habit of facing your fears.

5. Recognizing and Managing Resistance

Do not confuse these emotions with the feeling of butterflies. While they can be intimidating, those butterflies are beneficial because they help us prepare for what we're about to do. Emotions are a natural part of being human; they never go away. It's important to remember that everyone experiences them. However, understanding resistance, recognizing when it occurs, and knowing how to address it will empower you to overcome it.

In summarizing this chapter, whenever you take a principled stand in the face of adversity, it's inevitable that you will encounter resistance. This is especially true when you're pursuing something meaningful. The key is not to resist your emotions or internalize feelings of failure. Instead, process the experience in the moment, trust yourself, and move forward.

> *"The spirit of evil is a negation of the life force by fear. Only boldness can deliver us from fear. And if the risk is not taken, the meaning of life is violated. And that's a summons, accountability, to show up as best we can in the face of circumstances over which we may have no control over, whatsoever!"* - Carl Jung – On Transcending Fear

Open a New Room You Have Never Entered

As we conclude Chapter 2, remember that you are stepping into a completely new mental space, one your old self and previous patterns of thinking cannot follow. You're not just learning; you're transforming. With the foundation of a **Growth Mindset** now in place, and the tools to navigate **Resistance, Fear, and Failure** at your disposal, you're ready to move forward into the next stage of training. To help reinforce and personalize what you've learned, take a few moments to complete the questionnaire that follows.

Resistance, Fear, and Failure Questionnaire

Instructions:

Rate your agreement with each statement below using the following scale: Be honest—this is about self-awareness, not perfection.

1 = Never (0% of the time)
2 = Rarely (less than 25%)
3 = Sometimes (about 50%)
4 = Often (about 75%)
5 = Always (100%)

Section 1: Resistance

1.	I delay reaching out to prospects even when I know I should.	
2.	I second-guess my scripts or offers before hitting "send."	
3.	I avoid following up if I expect they might say "no."	
4.	I feel tension in my body before initiating cold calls.	
5.	I rehearse excessively instead of taking real action.	
6.	I find reasons to "prepare more" rather than engage directly.	
7.	I interpret silence from clients as a form of rejection.	
8.	I pull back when I sense hesitancy in a buyer.	
9.	I tell myself I'm "not ready" even when I am.	

Section 2: Fear

10.	I worry people will see me as pushy or manipulative.
11.	I fear sounding unqualified or unsure during a conversation.
12.	I avoid situations that could expose me to judgment.
13.	I fear being rejected more than I value being accepted.
14.	I worry that each "no" defines my ability to sell.
15.	I dread entering conversations where objections might arise.
16.	I hold back ideas because I'm afraid they'll be dismissed.
17.	I compare myself negatively to more experienced sellers.
18.	I fear looking unprepared—even if I am.

Section 3: Failure

19.	I view losing a sale as a personal failure.
20.	I replay failed conversations in my head long after they're over.
21.	I feel like quitting after a string of rejections.
22.	I rarely take time to review what I learned from a loss.
23.	I over-personalize outcomes beyond my control.
24.	I avoid setting bold goals to avoid failing publicly.
25.	I struggle to see failure as part of the growth process.

Scoring: (Total Possible Score: 25–125)

Add up your total score	

Score 25–49 / Low Resistance - *You show strong confidence and emotional resilience in sales situations. Fear and resistance have minimal influence on your actions. You actively face resistance, fear, and failure with awareness and resilience. Keep refining your growth mindset by mentoring others, practicing self-compassion, and exploring new strategies.*

Score 50–74 / Moderate Resistance - *You may experience occasional tension with rejection or a fear of failure and avoid discomfort at times. But you have the tools and self-awareness to navigate through it.*

Score 75–99 / High Resistance - *Resistance is actively influencing your sales process. You may be holding back out of fear, and this likely impacts your consistency and results. You likely operate within limits shaped by fear and resistance; it's time to challenge core narratives.*

Score 100–125 / Very High Resistance - *You're likely operating in a highly fear-driven state. Emotional blocks could be deeply rooted in self-worth, confidence, or past experiences. Consider seeking support from mentors or training that helps rebuild psychological safety. Be gentle with yourself and start small: celebrate tiny wins.*

CHAPTER 3
WORLD-CLASS MENTAL TOUGHNESS
THE DRIVING FORCE BEHIND TRANSFORMATION AND GROWTH

Until 1954, the prevailing belief was that humans could not run a mile in less than four minutes. However, that very year, English miler Roger Bannister shattered this belief. Doctors and scientists had deemed the four-minute barrier insurmountable, even suggesting that attempting to break it could be fatal. Bannister's words, *"When I got up from the track after collapsing at the finish line, I figured I was dead,"* underscore the enormity of his achievement. His story is a powerful testament that a self-limiting mindset can be the main obstacle to achieving what seems *impossible* in sports and business. Bannister's feat is a beacon of hope, a reminder that even the most daunting challenges can be conquered with the right mindset.

Let's begin by defining world-class mental toughness. Mental toughness isn't just resilience; it's repeatable resilience. Most people define mental toughness as the ability to push through pain or endure stress. But that's incomplete. Real mental toughness isn't about suppression; it's about structure. It's a refined inner system for handling pressure, navigating emotion, and executing under adversity with composure and clarity.

Mental determination is the driving force behind transformation. When your desire, purpose, and determination to succeed are stronger than your daily challenges or trials, you move the scales of mental strength and exercise mental toughness. This transformative power is within your reach, enabling you to excel in business. Whether it's overcoming a complex negotiation, leading a team through a crisis, or persisting in the face of market challenges, mental toughness is a high standard, a level of excellence top performers maintains to be the best.

I have always admired Navy SEALs for their extraordinary mental toughness and resilience. Becoming a SEAL requires enduring some of the most demanding military training in the world. When recruits first arrive, it is often impossible to tell which individual will succeed, as the training has an attrition rate of 80% to 90%.

To prepare for this training, candidates must run 40 miles a week, including 30% of that distance in boots, 20 miles on rugged terrain, and 10 miles on soft sand while wearing boots. Additionally, they perform 1,000 abdominal exercises daily and spend an hour swimming in cold water. This rigorous regimen tests every aspect of their survival capability. Out of a class of 250, only about 10 may successfully complete the training.

Importantly, SEAL training is only 20% physical and 80% focused on mental toughness. This means that most of the training emphasizes mental resilience rather than just physical endurance. Techniques such as self-meditation, self-visualization, and positive self-talk in challenging situations are essential for overcoming obstacles.

Mental toughness is an intrinsic quality that resides deep within us. It will keep men alive in elements that are not survivable. People have lifted ten times their weight to save a loved one. Athletes have endured insurmountable odds to win. Many veterans have returned from war after losing limbs, yet they find new purpose and set new goals. Mothers often work two jobs selflessly to give their children the best possible start. This is what mental toughness means! The power of purpose lies in having a clear vision of what you want to accomplish. The deeper your sense of purpose in life, the greater clarity and mental toughness you will find. Without a vision and purpose, you will aimlessly wander.

My primary sport growing up was wrestling; I started in 4th grade. I won my share of tournaments and a few Juniors Olympic titles. By the time I was a varsity wrestler in my first year of high school, I was well-versed in all the moves: freestyle throws, shucks, and takedowns. I had the opportunity to attend the NCAA wrestling championships one year in Seattle, Washington. These championships featured the best wrestlers in the country and some even went on to compete in the Olympics. I was eager to see moves I had never encountered before.

However, what I experienced over the two days was surprising. I didn't see any new or innovative moves. Instead, I witnessed the same techniques I had learned in 4th grade: double-leg takedowns, single-leg takedowns, reversals, and arm bars. I was taken aback, as I expected to see more advanced wrestling. But here's what I learned: it wasn't the fancy moves that distinguished these wrestlers as worldclass athletes. Their mindset and ability to execute the fundamentals of 4th-grade wrestling set them apart.

All the wrestlers used the same basic techniques; the difference lay in their effort, commitment, mental toughness, and execution skills. Their mental toughness was like granite, while their competitors were softer stones. I could imitate all their wrestling moves, but as in sales, anyone can be average. However, if you execute the fundamentals of who you are and your skill set at a world-class level, you can excel in the top 1% of what you do. So, let's start building this mindset.

"Success Lies in The Relentless Execution of The Basics" - Leonardo Da Vinci

Mental Toughness Must Be Stronger Than Daily Resistance

Why is mental toughness necessary? Every day, you are faced with cognitive challenges. Your opponent is resistance. Resistance is defined by how you respond to your life's internal and external forces, such as the demands of your job, the dynamics of your relationships, the fluctuations in your income, the scarcity of opportunities, etc. Life is challenging. It has a natural energy force that creates resistance. These outside forces are powerful. Without mental toughness and discipline, you are unprepared and moving towards mediocrity. A weak mindset produces a low energy frequency and cannot free themselves from being a pawn on the chessboard of resistance.

You can allow people or circumstances to author your life or take control. By developing mental strength like a powerful and versatile queen in chess, you can strategically influence your circumstances and the people around you on your life's chessboard, feeling secure and empowered.

The more mental strength you possess, the weaker your opposition becomes. You move this energy force where you want when grounded in mental toughness. Your true power lies in controlling your emotions, self-belief, self-control, commitment, determination, consistency, and purpose, which are the key strengths that generate mental toughness, making you feel confident and capable. They enable you to influence people and situations, helping you achieve your goals. Your mental toughness must surpass the daily challenges posed by resistance. Now, let's apply this mindset to sales.

How To Maintain Mental Toughness in Sales

What does it take to be mentally tough in sales? It is the ability to work hard and respond resiliently to failure and adversity, to organize, control, and regulate your emotions with the daily discipline to stay focused on your goal. People who can thrive under pressure, change and adapt when things are complicated, and maintain consistent effort until they see results produce mental toughness. This mindset is not just a tool; it's a way of life that inspires and motivates us to keep pushing forward.

This mindset of mental toughness empowers you to conquer daily challenges. Your mindset is the strongest tool in your arsenal to achieve your goal. However, the first hurdle for most salespeople is allowing everyday circumstances, distractions, and others to divert their attention, scattering their emotions and requiring more mental focus to manage this environment.

Sales become more complex if you don't have laser focus. The tendency to adopt a victim mentality can pull you in, leading to thoughts like, "I can't do it because," "They're to blame, not me." You will begin to make excuses for being incapable and wasting valuable time. You open a myriad of issues that are not necessary if you don't have a game plan each day in precisely what you want to achieve. The absence of mental toughness will compound challenges and negative thinking, neutralize your mindset and leave you unable to master adversity. You find yourself disorganized, reacting to stressors, ineffective, and feeling helpless.

If you have never considered your level of mental toughness, chances are you are not fully utilizing the mental strength you possess. Life is rarely smooth, but you must be mentally stronger than the circumstances you find yourself in. You must learn to regulate your feelings and emotions; if we don't have the power to regulate our feelings around a situation or an event, then that event has power over us as opposed to us over that moment.

The mindset of mental toughness requires you to respond to situations precisely and think in a specific way to produce the right attitudes when managing daily trials and challenges. Those with mental toughness possess an inner strength and resilience that surpass their natural talents and skills. This inner strength stems from self-confidence, the ability to manage negative thoughts, attention control, and goal visualization. It is fueled by motivation and enthusiasm, enabling individuals to maintain and attitude of self-belief even in the face of adversity.

These mental techniques and skills are necessary to become mentally tough. Peak performance requires mental strength. You need to recognize that your mental toughness will define your ability to succeed. A mindset that is not prepared for the challenges of life will fail. It takes a mindset built to battle the forces of challenge every day rather than surrendering to unproductive thoughts that sabotage your power to succeed.

You do not have to be more courageous, talented, or intelligent, just more consistent. One of the most powerful forces in life is consistency, being able to do something in repetition over and over again. Build systems for your daily sales duties, calls, time management, lead management, etc. Daily scheduled repetition is the framework and rails that produce consistency and will complement mental toughness. Your success won't come from what you do occasionally but from what you do consistently. Commitment gets you started, consistency gets you somewhere, and persistence keeps you going. Consistency turns average into excellence.

Discipline leads to habits. Habits leads to consistency; consistency leads to growth.

Summary of Mental Toughness in Life and Sales

Mental toughness is a personality trait. It's not a gene you are born with. It is a mindset that can be developed. But it is hard to define because it is a deep inner strength developed through purpose and experience. No two people live through challenges and adversity the same way. A person will find their path to mental toughness, some find it through personal tragedy, coming to deep self-reflection where they examine their values and judgments. It could be a trial or test that forces them to question who they are and what matters to them. Invariably, they emerge from that experience better and more self-confident, knowing their purpose and changing in some fundamental way.

Others are motivated to find mental toughness because they want to be the best at their work. However you get there, mental toughness is essential for success in sales and life. Without increasing your mental toughness, you will suffer in mediocrity. To stay mentally tough every day, thrive under pressure, perform, and survive at a high level, you must understand the complex balance of what activates mental toughness in you.

Top producers are not more intelligent or talented than anyone else but have the mental fortitude to overcome anything standing in their way of reaching their goal. This is the defining factor in succeeding in sales. When you reset mental toughness in sales, you are like an automatic machine. You commit and focus on how many calls, appointments, and presentations you make daily, weekly, and monthly. You are creating a daily sales system and utilizing time management to produce these results. Resistance or rejection does not stick. You focus on the process, not the outcome. Mental toughness powers this mindset. Anything worthwhile takes grit, determination, and learning to get out of your way to succeed. And the good news is you have way more potential in your mental strength than you might believe.

The primary distinction between a fixed mindset and mentally tough individuals is the results and actions they can achieve. They can manage a wide range of emotions while maintaining consistency through effort, driven by strong motivation and a positive attitude that inspires them.

10 Steps to Increase Mental Toughness

1. Increase Self-Awareness

By becoming more aware of the emotions that influence your thoughts, decisions, and actions, you can understand what drives you and work to eliminate any feelings that hinder your mental strength. This increased self-awareness can lead to better decision-making, improved communication, and stronger relationships with clients. By increasing your self-awareness of your emotions and behaviors, you will empower yourself and build greater confidence in your ability to sell your product and connect with your client.

2. Push Through Limits

Identify challenging areas in your life that make you uncomfortable. Embracing these difficult situations in business and personal life will encourage growth and prevent complacency. This practice can empower you, build self-confidence, and strengthen your mindset.

3. Learn to Control Your Mind

Keep a tight rein on your thoughts. Why? Because we become what we think. It's been said, "You can't stop a bird from landing on your head, but you can prevent it from building a nest." In other words, while negative thoughts may be unavoidable, you can choose not to dwell on them and let them take root. By changing your mindset about self-limiting beliefs and other obstacles, you can rewire your brain to work for you rather than against you.

4. Focus Your Center of Attention

Concentrate on the fundamental actions that lead to your success. Assess your daily tasks and take steps that produce results. Seek feedback and adjust as needed. Plan your time effectively and keep your goals in sight. Clearing your mind of unnecessary thoughts will help you concentrate on achieving results.

5. Mentally Tough People Pursue Growth

Mentally tough individuals are lifelong learners. They instinctively understand how to apply the lessons they've learned and recognize the importance of continually improving at tasks they already excel in. They realize that first place at the start does not guarantee finishing there. When they stumble, they see mistakes not as failures but as opportunities for growth. Life is a classroom, and with each lesson comes greater confidence in their ability to do better next time.

6. Live in Reality or Fact

Your perception can be either your power or your prison. Mental toughness strengthens when you fully engage with reality and facts. Living in denial is a state that diminishes your strength and can persist for a lifetime. It robs you of your potential. If you're in denial, you cannot fully feel or experience the true power of who you are.

Reality involves staying connected to your emotions. It means being willing to fail, not deflecting responsibility, avoiding excuses, taking full accountability, facing problems directly, and not allowing daily circumstances to control your life. By authentically experiencing both joy and sadness, you build mental strength by seeing things as they truly are, whether good or bad.

7. Start Small

Focus on achieving small goals, such as making a phone call, delivering a presentation, or arriving at work on time. Concentrate only on the next step in your day to reach a small goal. Ask yourself, "What's the next step?" and then act. Remember, you can't accomplish larger goals without first achieving these smaller ones.

8. Systems Complement Mental Toughness

Establish a framework for your job by defining specific duties, organizing your time, and implementing a daily system for calls, appointments, and presentations. Streamlining efforts enhances efficiency. Mentally resilient individuals create systems that enable focus despite life's challenges.

9. Purpose Activates Mental Toughness

Find your purpose by exploring your thoughts, beliefs, desires, and goals. Focusing on your purpose is essential, it is the titanium that drives mental toughness. Your emotions work in a domino effect. When they are in order and aligned with your purpose, you compound mental strength to achieve your goal.

10. Emotional Intelligence

Emotional intelligence is critical in producing mental toughness. We will cover this in chapter 5.

"It all starts with who you are - I always tell our players, who you are is more important than what you do. How high you jump - how fast you run, because who you are is your character - and your character is an accumulation of your thoughts - your habits and your priorities on a day-to-day basis - because those 3 things determine the choices you make, and the choices you make, make who you are. Good guy bad guy - hard working, lazy - responsible, irresponsible, and it takes a certain amount of discipline to do what you are supposed to do - when you are supposed to do it, - the way it supposed to get done." - Nick Sabin

Open a New Room You Have Never Entered

As we conclude chapter 3, remember that you are transforming your mindset into a space you have never experienced before. The old you and your previous ways of thinking cannot remain in this room. You are becoming comfortable in this new environment and developing a fresh perspective.

You now have the foundation of a **Growth Mindset:** five steps to manage **Resistance, Fear, and Failure** and ten steps to elevate your **Mental Toughness**. Begin incorporating these values and beliefs into your daily life. Move through this space throughout your day and apply these principles wherever possible.

Mental Toughness Questionnaire

Instructions:

Rate your agreement with each statement below using the following scale: Be honest—this is about self-awareness, not perfection.

1 = Always (100%)
2 = Often (about 75%)
3 = Sometimes (about 50%)
4 = Rarely (less than 25%)
5 = Never (0% of the time)

Section 1: Drive and Determination

1.	I am determined to succeed.	
2.	Do you persevere?	
3.	Do you visualize what you don't have but hope for and work towards what you want?	
4.	When you feel there is no reason to believe it will happen, do you have the faith to work harder?	
5.	Do you believe you can?	
6.	Are you willing to work harder than anyone else?	
7.	Are you willing to sacrifice time, energy, and effort at all costs to meet your goal?	
8.	I have a deep commitment to succeed at work.	
9.	I desire to be the best at what I do.	
10.	I'm willing to do what others won't to succeed.	
11.	When I don't reach my goal, it makes me want to try harder.	
12.	I believe I have the power to change my circumstances.	
13.	I have more potential in my effort to give more.	

Section 2: Emotional Control & Focus

14.	Do your emotions stay in a challenge or give up easily?	
15.	I make good decisions under pressure.	
16.	When I make mistakes, I can maintain focus on what's next.	
17.	I can control my emotions when working.	
18.	I can manage my emotions when things don't go as planned.	
19.	I can control distracting thoughts when working to stay on task.	
20.	I don't lose sight of my daily goal when under stress.	
21.	Are you in control of your actions and emotions?	
22.	My strength lies in my ability to manage how I respond to what is happening, both in my actions and emotions.	

Section 3: Resilience & Recovery

23.	I don't give up even when the odds are against me.	
24.	I don't lose belief in myself when I fail.	
25.	I can overcome self-doubt when it comes.	
26.	I understand my potential is limited by how I think.	

Section 4: Courage & Self-Belief

27.	I am willing to face my fears.	
28.	I am not afraid of others and what they think of me.	
29.	I am a leader in my work and among those who know me.	
30.	I do not giveaway my power to others.	

Scoring: (Total Possible Score: 30–150)

Add up your total score	

Score 30–60 / Mentally Tough - *This range indicates a strong command over emotional resilience, concentration, and the ability to remain composed in high-pressure situations. You likely demonstrate a proactive approach to challenges, turning obstacles into fuel for growth and rebounding quickly from setbacks; your emotional regulation and sense of purpose act as steady internal anchors.*

Score 61–90 / Developing Mental Toughness - *In this range, you have cultivated meaningful tools, such as discipline, perseverance, and readiness to bounce back. However, you may still experience moments of hesitation, inconsistency, or difficulty with emotional regulation. These fluctuations suggest that while your mindset is on solid footing, there are specific "pressure points" that could benefit from refinement.*

Score 91–120 / Emerging Awareness - *This score indicates that you're in a self-discovery zone, becoming aware of how your mindset influences your outcomes. Challenges such as inner criticism, low self-esteem, or performance anxiety can feel overwhelming at times. But this range is packed with potential: awareness is the threshold of growth.*

Score 121–150 / Needs Focus (Foundational Growth) - *A score in this range doesn't reflect failure. It reflects untapped capacity. Mental toughness may feel distant, but that's precisely why this stage matters most. You may be experiencing frequent feelings of overwhelm, a lack of motivation, or difficulty recovering from stress. The good news? This is where transformation begins. Self-kindness and structure will carry you much farther than pressure or shame. There's powerful growth available here when you permit yourself to take one intentional step at a time.*

CHAPTER 4
WORLD-CLASS ATTITUDE
THE OPERATING SYSTEM OF ELITE PERFORMANCE

World-class attitude is the engineered emotional climate that governs identity-driven execution, regardless of external conditions. It's not a mood. It's a structured mindset architecture designed to sustain clarity, consistency, and composure, especially when results, recognition, or rhythm are missing. Most people treat attitude as a mood swing. But elite performers design it as a system that is reliable, responsive, and rooted in identity rather than emotional weather. It's how you choose to operate when the world isn't cooperating.

The power of your mindset is key in shaping the actions of your attitude. To build a world-class attitude, we must first clarify the difference between a person's mindset and attitude. Your mindset is how you perceive the world, 24/7, through your values, history, experiences, and deep-seated beliefs of how you live your life. It acts as a lens through which we interpret our experiences and challenges. For instance, a growth mindset is characterized by believing that abilities can be developed through dedication, hard work, and open-mindedness to promote change. It influences our ability to learn and grow. If you lack self-confidence, doubt your abilities, and hold back from your true potential, it's a sign that you're not fully embracing your capabilities. By altering your fixed beliefs about yourself, you can transform your self-perception and how you present yourself to the world. This transformation begins with a shift in your mindset, offering a hopeful path to self-improvement.

However, your attitude is part of your mindset and governs your actions. How you experience situations, people, places, or things will shape your attitude more than your mindset. Your attitude is a temporary feeling or disposition toward specific situations or people. It can change from moment to moment based on experiences, emotions, and context. While mindset is generally stable, attitude can vary widely. Attitude is not just a thought or feeling; it's a visible manifestation of your beliefs and actions. You might declare, 'I will no longer perceive people that way, but your attitude only changes when you start behaving and treating them differently.

By developing a robust growth mindset, we can navigate life's challenges with greater confidence and adaptability while maintaining an awareness of our attitudes, which allows us to respond constructively to various circumstances. Understanding these distinctions enhances our self-awareness and empowers us to foster healthier relationships and pursue personal and professional excellence more effectively.

It's a well-known saying that your attitude is the barometer of your success, and there is profound truth in that. Your attitude is the sculptor of the beliefs held within your mindset, whether those beliefs are positive or negative. However, accepting the pillars of truth about yourself and your identity will elevate your attitude. Let's look at a man with an exceptional attitude and why he was the best of all time.

Never Personalize Failure or Make It Apart of Your Identity

I want to begin by talking about the legendary Jack Nicklaus, widely regarded as the greatest golfer of all time. He described his mindset as having a jar filled with positive thoughts. If he made a bad shot, he would quickly dismiss it from his mind and focus on the next one. Even before a bad shot landed, he was already thinking about how to solve the problem of his next shot. He never allowed himself to say, "I played poorly today," "It's just not my day," or "I'm no good."

Jack never let failure, or a bad shot impact the success of his next shot. He could do this because he refused to personalize failure or let it define him. Instead, he viewed failure as a challenge to address and solve in the moment.

His competitors could not process failure, pressure, and challenges in the same way. These factors often overwhelmed their ability to perform at their best. Jack won 18 majors, the most by any golfer in history, and finished second 19 times in major golf championships, which only featured four majors each year.

No one has come close to matching this record. His mindset was rooted in his self-belief, while his attitude reflected how he approached the game through his actions and effort. Although he may not have been the most technically skilled golfer, he possessed the best mindset and attitude in the sport. He remained focused in the moment, always looking ahead for solutions.

Turn The Kaleidoscope You're Looking Through

The key to maintaining a productive attitude is to visualize the next step when things go wrong. You don't need to carry the baggage of the past into the present. There's no reason to engage in negative self-talk, such as, "I am so bad at this," or "This always happens to me." Your thoughts and words have the power to shape your reality. Instead of judging your emotions which can be complex and overwhelming, focus on the best action you can take and then follow through with it. A negative attitude can develop gradually, leading to significant emotional stress.

Several factors contribute to this shift, including mistakes, regrets, missed opportunities, circumstances beyond our control, unexpected family deaths, and the challenges of living paycheck to paycheck. All these difficulties can impede our ability to realize our full potential. Over the years, self-doubt can take root, along with thoughts about what might have been. Additionally, when someone you trust tells you that you will never amount to anything, it can significantly impact your self-esteem.

Life changing events can significantly influence your mindset and attitude. Over time, feelings of despair, compromise, resentment, and self-doubt may become ingrained habits. You may find yourself believing that everyone owes you something, leading to increased irritability and depression. This isn't a reality you have to accept. You have the freedom to grow; the potential has always been within you. However, if you can't see or believe in it, settling for less in life becomes easier. You weren't born with this mindset and attitude; it develops over time through your choices and decisions. It's easier to succeed and find happiness when you have a strong, resilient attitude that confronts daily problems and challenges. If you're not emotionally and mentally stronger than the obstacles you face or the competition you encounter, you risk missing the opportunity to be your best. Transitioning from a negative mindset to a more productive one is not an insurmountable leap.

This chapter focuses on the kaleidoscope you're looking through, shifting your perspective ever so slightly, allowing for greater clarity as you recognize the potential and emotional strength inherent in your attitude. However, you must be willing to let go of your current mental programming. Any excuses or denial will undermine your ability to embrace and understand the foundational truths that can elevate your attitude to a world-class level. Now, let's establish the framework for this attitude.

Responsibility
The Foundation of a World-Class Attitude

Scott Hamilton, the Olympic skater, once said, "The only disability in life is a bad attitude." A world-class attitude is built on taking full responsibility, while a bad attitude arises from a victim mentality. When you consistently view life through the lens of "it's not my fault" or "there's nothing that can help," and blame challenges on others, you are operating from a victim mindset. This mind is set, as the term suggests. No one consciously chooses to be a victim; it's not a condition or a disease. People adopt this mentality because it provides a way to cope with life, an emotional payoff that only they can change. This attitude keeps individuals trapped in mediocrity, offering only a false hope of achieving success. So, how does one develop their attitude? Your attitude is shaped by your emotions, experiences, learned behaviors, habits, and the choices you make.

Your mindset shapes your character, encompassing who you are, your beliefs, values, principles, and purpose in life. It influences how you live your life. Your attitude affects how you execute your daily activities, your personal and professional performance, and your ability to overcome challenges and achieve your goals. Again, your mindset is the foundation of your attitude. The health of your mindset, (beliefs, open-mindedness, mental flexibility, perspective, etc.) directly impacts your attitude. The more power you produce in your mindset, the more effective your attitude will be in executing actions and achieving results. In previous chapters, we focused on developing the healthy fundamentals of a World-Class Mindset, specifically a growth mindset. Now is the time to apply what we've learned to improve your attitude. You face many daily challenges, such as resistance, stress, worry, doubt, calls to make, and pressure to produce. These difficulties can test your attitude and leave you feeling at the mercy of your circumstances. If you let these circumstances control your mindset and overwhelm your attitude, you risk neutralizing your actions and efforts, which can lead to mediocrity. Over time, the growing mountain of problems can render your mindset and attitude ineffective, turning you into a slave to your circumstances. To thrive, your attitude must protect your mindset's plans, beliefs, and purpose as you work towards your goals. The key to achieving this is to recognize that your attitude needs to be rooted in self-awareness.

Attitude is Rooted in Self-awareness

A world-class attitude is a natural trait grounded in self-awareness. It allows you to assess situations accurately and acts as a guiding force during challenges and adversity. Use it as intended to make the most of your attitude, letting it inspire and empower you. This is the purpose of your attitude: not to defeat you. You can retrain your brain's habits to adopt this mindset. Habits shape our identity. Any negative thought that arises (aside from primal fear) is either an illusion of fear or a lie, distracting you from the truth. The truth will always offer options to help you move forward. Negative thoughts can bind and limit you, preventing you from seeing things as they truly are.

What is biblical truth? It is defined as "truth consistent with the mind, will, character, glory, and being of God." More specifically, "Truth is the self-expression of God." This definition captures the essence of the biblical understanding of truth. In secular terms, truth is described as "the quality or state of being true."

You have the freedom to choose which definition of truth to follow. Embracing truth allows for a more accurate understanding of reality, helping you recognize your strengths and weaknesses, manage circumstances, your ability to produce results, and connect to the power and purpose of your life. Living your life through the lens of truth helps you become the best version of yourself. It eliminates self-denial, clears away ineffective emotions, and keeps you grounded in authenticity and humility toward others. You need not worry about pretense or trying to appear perfect; when you embrace the truth of who you are, you realize you are more than adequate. You gain acceptance and respect because others see your authenticity and are inspired to seek it for themselves.

Why are elite producers regarded as the best of the best? Have you ever considered this? It starts with truth. You must be truthful with yourself about your actions. Are you putting in the hard work? Are you adequately prepared? Is your time management in line with the results you expect? Are your skills sufficient for the job? Are you taking the necessary steps to be the best you can be? Don't let delusion cloud your mindset. Remember, hard work and preparation are essential to unlocking your potential.

How many salespeople are truly honest when self-assessing their efforts? Are you aware of what needs to be done and take responsibility for your job, or do you sometimes justify your shortcomings? When you don't meet your quota, make mistakes, or fail to follow through, do you find excuses for why it happened? For example, have you evaluated your sales strategy after a failed presentation or reflected on your time management when you missed a deadline? Self-assessment is not about finding fault but about empowering yourself to take control of your professional growth.

Remember that the most successful individuals are where they are because they are honest with themselves. They understand who they are and how they prepare, work, and challenge themselves. They don't shy away from the truth, which sets them apart. So, where do you stand? It's time to ask yourself that question. This mindset and attitude will also produce other strengths while reinforcing responsibility, mental toughness, and emotional intelligence. The more you live authentically, the healthier your emotional mindset and attitude will become.

Is your attitude based on truth? Truth aligns with facts and reality. A world-class attitude evaluates the truth of situations with an unbiased perspective, viewing them as problems to be solved. By assessing truth in any circumstance, you remain grounded and better interpret perceived reality, setting aside conflicting emotions. Choose a "truth" to live by, recognizing that truth can be subjective for each individual. However, the strength of your mindset is key to how you interpret and process your circumstances. What you think, see, do, and experience are all conditions that happen to you, which you can process through your mindset and attitude, making you more aware and conscious.

Truth Will Elevate Your Attitude

When you learn to identify and live truthfully, you become more assertive in facing daily challenges and adversity. Truth is not just a virtue, but a frequency that flows and prospers in business, relationships, and finances. It brings out the best in you and those around you. Adopting this mindset will enhance your performance and strengthen your interpersonal skills. This transformation will improve how you present yourself, what you say, and how you communicate, ultimately attracting others to you.

It's a fact, challenges and difficulties will always test your attitude. However, here's the empowering truth: if you recognize this beforehand, your mindset will shift, making you mentally stronger and better prepared to face those trials. It's important to recognize that individuals with a world-class attitude are not immune to pain, defeat, complex challenges, or negative emotions; they are grounded in the reality of the situation.

A great attitude isn't simply about wearing a smile every day. It involves maintaining an optimistic outlook, even amidst chaos. High achievers can thrive in turbulent situations because they possess the mental flexibility to adapt and persevere. They remain calm and do not let themselves become flustered, allowing them to manage their emotions effectively.

They understand that none of us can control what life brings. They recognize that focusing on the past consumes valuable time in the present. Life is ongoing and will continue to test their resolve, character, and fortitude in the days ahead. They know that success in both life and sales occur when they can reduce resistance within themselves, empowering them to be in control while dealing with others. They maintain a reality-based perception of themselves and their goals. By accepting failure, they learn and move closer to success.

Their attitude is driven not by arrogance or a false identity but by a deep sense of humility, authenticity, and self-awareness. Serving others with the universal language of care, concern, and love, they present themselves with trust and integrity, fully aware of who they are and reflecting that to those around them. They are relentless optimists, believing that things will improve through faith and continuous effort if given the chance. This faith is not blind; it is a conviction in the power of consistent effort and a positive attitude to overcome challenges.

A clear plan and purpose define a world-class attitude. Individuals with this mindset are determined to achieve their daily, monthly, and long-term goals. They recognize that the only threat to their intentions and purpose is the fluctuating nature of their attitude. Therefore, they are committed to safeguarding it at all costs. They operate from a proven mindset fueled by emotions that drive their success: excitement, determination, energy, focus, enthusiasm, motivation, discipline, persistence, and hope.

They utilize these emotional tools daily to sustain and enhance their attitude, intention, and purpose. These tools can be developed through consistent practice and self-reflection. Healthy emotions that drive success are not activated without a clear plan, purpose, and goals. In sales, you must be able to fire yourself up daily and motivate yourself emotionally, just as an athlete does before the competition.

10 Steps Maintaining a World-Class Attitude

1. Don't Allow Problems to Accumulate

Allowing problems to accumulate will continually test the strength of your fortitude and weaken your attitude over time. When you have a problem or challenge, take care of it now! If they're intermediate to long-term issues, plan how you will manage them at the appointed time and then let it go. Never allow negative thinking to simmer; do what you can now and move on.

2. Action Solves Problems

Never let your mood dictate what you do. When negative emotions like worry, concern, fear, and anxiety show up, you'll feel better by acting rather than meditating on the stew of your problems. Action not only activates creativity but also empowers you to solve problems. You minimize worry and concern when you stay positive and direct your energy, feeling more in control and confident.

3. Identify Negative Thoughts

When negative thoughts arise, recognize they are an illusion of fear, misleading you from the truth. The truth always provides options to move forward. Negative thoughts limit your thinking and prevent you from seeing things as they are.

4. Identify Truth in Your Actions

Break through false emotional barriers that prevent you from realizing the truth of who you are. When you are in denial, lack a solid work ethic, are unwilling to take full responsibility, or cannot self-assess yourself honestly, you hinder your ability to build a world-class attitude.

5. Life Is a Classroom

When facing trials and challenges, see negative experiences and challenges as opportunities to grow, extract the value and lesson, then let it go. Difficult situations are never fun in the heat of the battle, but they will strengthen your resolve and make you better. Life is a classroom of learning through our trials, fostering a sense of resilience and optimism as you grow and learn.

6. Fill the Jar

Train your mind to think positively when selling on the phone, managing your business, or talking with a client. The more self-aware you are, operating from positive emotions, the more power you produce. Your mind is ten times more powerful when you think positively, developing and building the framework that breeds mental and emotional strength. Imagine your mind as a jar, and each positive thought as a marble that fills it. The more marbles you add, the more your mind is filled with positivity, and the less room there is for mental baggage that carries self-doubt and low self-confidence, fear, and insecurity. The longer you stay and practice this mindset, the more it becomes the attitude you operate from.

7. See the Next Shot

When things go wrong, be in the present moment while looking for the next solution. This is like being on a tennis court, always ready for the next shot. Train your mind to be positive, adjust, and stay focused through adversity. Instead of dwelling on the problem, focus on the next step you can take to overcome it. This proactive mindset will help you maintain a positive attitude even in challenging situations.

8. Utilize Emotional Boosters

This is the gas needed to fuel and maintain the energy of your attitude daily, weekly, and long-term. Emotional boosters are like high-octane fuel for your mindset. Passionate, determined, enthusiastic, motivated, disciplined, persistent, and hopeful are all examples of emotional boosters. These emotions produce the visual of success before you get there. Neuroscience says that you begin to change your brain to look like that experience has already happened.

Life is a long desert road, and it takes time to reach the desired destination. Without emotional boosters along the way, you'll run out of gas and be just another person who gave up alongside the road. People always plan to succeed when they start. It happens when their resistance, despair, and negative thinking become stronger than their plan to succeed. Figure out what emotions ignite your excitement for work and life, and they will fuel your goals to achieve.

9. Use Your Attitude for What It Is Meant to Do!

Use your attitude as a coaching system. Allow it to inspire and strengthen you. Operating from a growth mindset, maintaining mental toughness, and staying self-aware of your emotions and the emotions of others produce a perspective and mindset of strength. Your attitude is the control center of your success. Learn to protect it against the arrows of challenge each day.

10. Write Your Strategy to Succeed

Having daily, weekly, and long-term goals is the road map of where you're going. Without a plan, purpose, and goals, the healthy emotions we just talked about that drive success are not activated. A well-executed game plan produces the will to succeed. A world-class attitude will help you overcome challenges, disappointments, failures, and trials, keeping you focused and determined on your path to success.

In summarizing chapter 4, incorporating these steps and exercises into your daily routine can significantly contribute to your success and improve your mental and emotional preparedness. By actively practicing these principles, you'll enhance your abilities, talent, skills, work ethic, and beliefs in all areas of your life. As you begin to value yourself more and treat yourself with kindness and respect, you will notice a positive shift in your confidence and overall resilience and attitude.

Open a New Room You Have Never Entered

In finishing this chapter, remember you are continuing to transform your mindset into a new space. It's new, the old, you cannot enter this room. The only thing that can enter and originate from this space are the principles of this book. You now have the bedrock foundation of a; **Growth Mindset**, 5 Steps in **Managing Resistance, Fear, and Failure**, 10 steps in strengthening **Mental Toughness,** 10 principles in maintaining a **World-Class Attitude**. Build and expand the values and principles in this book, stay in this room, and begin to think, feel and own the emotions and mindset you have learned.

Attitude Sales Questionnaire

Instructions: Rate your agreement with each statement below using the following scale: Be honest—this is about self-awareness, not perfection.

1 = Always (100%)
2 = Often (about 75%)
3 = Sometimes (about 50%)
4 = Rarely (less than 25%)
5 = Never (0% of the time)

Section 1: Self-Belief & Confidence

1.	I believe in my ability to close sales even in tough markets.	
2.	I view sales rejections as opportunities to learn and grow.	
3.	I maintain a positive mindset regardless of my sales performance.	
4.	I radiate confidence when interacting with prospects.	
5.	I consistently celebrate small wins.	

Section 2: Mindset & Motivation

6.	I stay motivated even when prospects show little interest.	
7.	I believe that consistent effort will lead to better sales outcomes.	
8.	I bounce back quickly from a lost deal or customer pushback.	
9.	I view sales as a craft I can continually improve through practice.	
10.	I remain enthusiastic throughout my sales day.	

Section 3: Communication & Empathy

11.	I actively listen to understand my client's true needs.	
12.	I empathize with client concerns, even when it delays the sale.	
13.	I stay composed and optimistic during tough conversations.	
14.	I adjust my tone and message based on the prospect's mood.	
15.	I leave every interaction with the client feeling respected and heard.	

Section 4: Resilience & Discipline

16.	I follow up consistently without losing energy or motivation.	
17.	I manage my time and prioritize tasks with intention.	
18.	I view pressure as fuel rather than stress.	
19.	I bounce back from consecutive losses without discouragement.	
20.	I maintain daily sales routines even when results don't show immediately.	

Section 5: Growth Orientation

21.	I seek feedback to improve, even when it's uncomfortable.	
22.	I believe my attitude influences my clients' trust in me.	
23.	I embrace change and adapt quickly to the sales process.	
24.	I regularly reflect on how my attitude affects my performance.	
25.	I invest time in building a resilient, growth-focused mindset.	

Scoring: (Total Possible Score: 25–125)

Add up your total score	

Score 25-49 / Inspirational Sales Attitude - *You exemplify a powerful growth-oriented mindset. Optimism, resilience, and consistency are deeply ingrained in your daily routine. Your energy likely uplifts your clients, and you recover swiftly from setbacks. Continue building on this momentum by considering mentoring others or documenting what works for you.*

Score 50-74 / Strong and Adaptive Sales Attitude - *You're doing a lot right. You approach challenges with a mostly healthy mindset; you view selling as a relationship-building opportunity, show enthusiasm, and adapt your approach to different clients. You likely lead with curiosity. However, a few patterns may be reactive instead of intentional, like disengaging after a rejection or struggling to stay motivated mid-cycle. Focusing on one or two areas for habit shifts could rapidly elevate your performance.*

Score 75-99 / Solid Foundation with Room to Grow - *Demonstrates a generally positive sales attitude with moments of self-doubt or disengagement under pressure. You might see-saw between enthusiasm and discouragement or rely on external wins to boost your attitude. Sees value in sales but doesn't fully own the identity. This is the sweet spot for reframing techniques, mindset training, and micro-habit changes. Self-awareness is your gateway, lean into it.*

Score 100-114 / Uncertain or Developing Sales Attitude - *Negative self-talk, inconsistency, or emotional fatigue may be influencing your sales interactions. Beginning to recognize the importance of a positive attitude but struggles to find authenticity in the sales role. You may over-personalize rejection or struggle to maintain resilience.*

Score 115-125 / Resistant or Negative Sales Attitude - *Your mindset may be actively interfering with your sales process. May view selling as manipulative, uncomfortable with persuasion, or skep-*

tical about value creation. Likely disengaged or anxious about customer interaction. If left unaddressed, discouragement, avoidance, or burnout could become patterns. The great news? This is where transformation begins. Even small shifts in belief can unlock energy and performance.

CHAPTER 5
WORLD-CLASS EMOTIONAL INTELLIGENCE
EMOTIONS AREN'T OBSTACLES—THEY'RE OPERATING INSTRUCTIONS

Emotions aren't noise; they're the raw material of your presence. This chapter explores how emotional awareness can become strategic precision, fostering deeper connections with clients, teammates, and oneself without compromising authenticity. Understanding oneself becomes the foundation for influence, clarity, and peak performance.

Let's begin by asking the question. What is emotional intelligence in sales? It's an awareness of your inner world, emotions, beliefs, values, and how you present yourself. It is recognizing your emotions and understanding what they tell you. It also involves your perception of your prospects and how they feel. No matter what situation they find themselves in, emotionally intelligent salespeople always know what to say and how to say it. This allows them to connect quickly with their prospects. This skill empowers both the salesperson and the prospect, presenting a sense of control and confidence in their interactions.

Mental toughness and a world-class attitude act as protective walls against the adversities and daily challenges you encounter, enabling you to combat negativity while pursuing your sales goals. Emotional intelligence serves as the thinker, planner, strategist, diplomat, and psychologist within your fortress, influencing the outcomes of your battles. It is your strategic tool, guiding every move and decision you make on the sales battlefield. Your success depends on your ability to manage your emotions and those of others through the various challenges, attitudes, and stresses that leaders face.

As mentioned in a previous chapter, a study by Cal Berkeley found that humans express 27 distinct emotional states, which is more complex than the previously believed six. This underscores the complex mindset necessary when presenting ourselves and our product in sales. You are an emotional being selling to another who has emotions, the key is finding mutual positive emotions that will keep them engaged while you deliver the sale. Disrupting the sales flow can be a result of errors, inappropriate comments, poorly received jokes, or a dull presentation. Your selling ability is directly influenced by the number and type of mistakes you make, whether technical, emotional, conscious, or unconscious. Top performers are keenly aware of this and rarely commit these errors, while average salespeople often remain unaware of their mistakes, causing potential buyers to feel uncomfortable.

The question arises: why are these mistakes made at all? Professional sales are less about the product itself; it's assumed that people want it. That desire is the only reason they will give you their time. The success of a sale relies on your self-awareness in how you present yourself, your ability to read the prospect, and your talent for engaging their emotions throughout the sales process. If this process is mishandled, the sale will not happen. However, if executed correctly, closing the sale becomes a mere formality.

First, we must identify the emotions that activate and enhance the sales process. The moment you shake hands; you share energy with your prospect, this is where emotions come into play. You experience an immediate awareness as your emotional sensors engage through the handshake and eye contact. Both of you are assessing your feelings and looking for a comfortable connection. Whether the emotions are positive or negative, you mirror each other's feelings. Your goal is to convey and demonstrate understanding and empathy, essentially resting your feelings in the other person's experience.

What emotions are you conveying? Your demeanor significantly influences your clients. Are you projecting confidence, credibility, character, product knowledge, energy, and enthusiasm? Or do you come across as unsure, nervous, controlled, intimidated, negative, or pretentious? You have the power to create a welcoming environment for your clients and are responsible for ensuring they feel comfortable from the moment they arrive.

People are a blank canvas when you first meet them, they often feel apprehensive but are generally willing to give you the benefit of the doubt, things will go well. By mirroring your emotions, you transfer your thoughts and feelings onto their blank canvas, showcasing your emotional state. You will begin to shape their perception as you interact based on your thoughts and actions. If executed well, they are on board and trust the connection, allowing you to take control of the interaction. Let's explore the skills that enhance emotional intelligence in sales.

Internal and External Self-awareness

Sales are unique because your emotional skills directly influence your personal and professional performance. You are the product! Prospects will only purchase once they first believe in your competence and style. Specific emotional attributes are imperative to mastering a world-class emotional intelligence in sales.

Your ability to understand, listen, communicate, empathize, identify, evaluate, express emotions, and lead are qualities for exceptional sales skills. So, how can we enhance these abilities? While everyone is born with varying levels of emotional intelligence (EQ), we can improve our skills through the powerful tool of self-awareness. When coupled with persistence, practice, and a deeper understanding of our behaviors, this allows us to raise our emotional intelligence. To do so, we must first break down the fundamentals of this mindset.

In his article for the Harvard Business Review, Anthony K. Tjan discusses the importance of self-awareness for leaders. He emphasizes that self-awareness is a common trait among successful entrepreneurs, managers, leaders, and salespeople. It is the key to identifying your strengths and weaknesses, what he calls your 'Superpowers' and your 'Kryptonite.' This understanding allows you to leverage your strengths while addressing your weaknesses, ultimately making you a more effective salesperson. As Tony Robbins stated, "If there is a rare quality in life, it is self-awareness. Self-awareness involves recognizing the difference between yourself and your patterns and understanding how those patterns impact the people around you."

The foundation of emotional intelligence is a strong sense of self-awareness. Dating back to 300 BC and the teachings of Greek philosophy, the idea of 'Know Thyself' has been a guiding principle for humanity. Self-awareness involves a deep understanding of your emotions and how your feelings influence your actions and interactions with others. By becoming more mindful of how your emotions can affect those around you, you become a more considerate, responsible, and effective salesperson.

In sales, however, there are two areas of focus. The first, internal self-awareness, this provides insight into our purpose, motivation, goals, manage our work environment, how we process our responsibilities, behaviors, and understanding our strengths, and weaknesses, as they directly influence our level of performance.

The second, is external self-awareness. This pertains to how others perceive us. It involves how we present ourselves, our ability to read buyers, our tone of voice, listening skills, and verbal and non-verbal communication skills, including eye contact and the emotions we express or fail to express. Professional sales are a process that requires both internal and external self-awareness.

Your capacity to excel largely depends on how well you navigate the chess game of sales. The buyer has the upper hand at the outset because they hold the final decision. Your role is to skillfully navigate the emotional and technical landmines of the sale, making strategic moves that benefit both you and the buyer.

Connecting, presenting effectively, decompressing fear and anxiety, building trust, and answering questions and objections so well, he is willing to take a player off the board each time to defend his position. As you enhance your internal and external self-awareness, you develop the foundational elements of world-class emotional intelligence in your personal and professional life. You become increasingly confident in your sales approach by honing your emotional skills and product knowledge. Now, let's explore how to apply this understanding to the practical aspects of sales.

Three Primary Areas to Improve Emotional Intelligence in Sales

1. Connecting with the Buyer

At the beginning of every sale, emotionally aware salespeople can lock into verbal and non-verbal communication much like a frequency; they tailor their words and actions to connect emotionally with the buyer. People are inherently wired to trust those they can identify with. The longer it takes to establish a connection and gain their confidence, the slimmer the chances of closing the sale. High-performance selling is straightforward if you are skilled at identifying what you are looking for. Whether you are on the phone or giving a presentation, every buyer has an emotional flow and rhythm, like a river, that indicates how they want to proceed.

Average salespeople often find themselves working against the buyer's natural tendencies, which can create resistance in the sales process. Buyers typically reveal their social dynamics through their behavior, allowing you to interpret their emotional cues by observing their personality, eye contact, and manner of speaking. These cues manifest in various ways, such as tone, intensity, body language, and personal styles—like know-it-all, sarcastic, sensitive, impatient, passive, or extroverted. These social-emotional styles have been developed over the years and reflect how individuals are comfortable presenting themselves. Once you identify a buyer's style, you can then adapt your approach accordingly. By doing so, you can reduce resistance and align your methods with their preferences for a more effective sales interaction.

2. How to Manage Questions & Objections

The true test of your selling ability and emotional intelligence lies in gaining your customers' trust, alleviating their fears and anxieties, and effectively addressing their questions and objections. These elements are like the first down markers on the football field of sales. Your ability to articulate and respond to questions and objections distinguishes average salespeople from top producers. Handling these situations is an excellent measure of your aptitude, skill, and product knowledge and your capacity to convey trust and integrity while helping others recognize the value and benefits of what you're selling.

When you successfully overcome each question and objection, you effectively neutralize the prospect's defense mechanisms, allowing you to advance the ball down the field. However, this is often where average salespeople become stuck, much like a deer caught in headlights. They lack the skills to secure a critical first down in the sale, leaving the buyer with an unsatisfactory or incomplete answer.

When salespeople are unprepared, they often lose emotional momentum. Responding ineffectively can result in a 15-yard penalty, making scoring harder. However, addressing questions and objections presents a valuable opportunity to make a significant impact, like completing a 50-yard pass. Capitalizing on these moments is pivotal rather than providing superficial answers that yield only a minimal 3-yard gain. Completing a 50-yard pass requires thorough preparation and well-thought-out, strategic responses, which empower you to take control of the game.

Questions and objections are valuable opportunities to clarify and illustrate the personalized benefits of owning the product to the buyer. Using a story or an example cannot only strengthen your response but also make it more engaging and memorable for the client. Not every question or objection will allow for this, but it's important to be prepared for when the opportunity arises. Effectively answering questions and objections while clients consider their thoughts, decisions, and judgments will help them feel more at ease and connect with you.

One common mistake I observe is that many salespeople respond to questions or objections too quickly or rely on the product to sell itself. It's beneficial to take the time and craft each answer to visually highlight and maximize the product's value, service, and ownership. Elite producers are not reactive but proactive. They have prepared answers to anticipated questions and objections before being raised, just as a football coach knows all the X's and O's and plays before the game starts.

3. Lead Presentation from Behind

Over the years, I have observed salespeople making the mistake of getting too far ahead of the prospect. They often disclose information too quickly during their presentation or attempt to close the deal at the wrong moment. Conversely, some are too slow to get to the point, which can create impatience in the prospect. This misalignment in the sales sequence raises a red flag for the buyer, leading them to say, "I want to think about it."

Every presentation has a natural rhythm that you must sense. If the prospect does not understand what you are sharing or explaining at any point in the presentation, and you move on to the next point prematurely, you have fumbled the ball. This weakens your ability to make the sale. You create two emotional timelines: yours and theirs. If the prospect gets lost in your presentation, they may express their hesitation by saying, "I want to think about it."

When you lead the sale from behind, by asking substantive questions and listening, you let the client create the sale and allow them to put the colors of concerns and needs on the canvas of the product. Then, you develop a beautiful mural for the buyer using their questions and objections, along with the benefits and features of the product. This is the art of selling. You allow the buyer to synchronize the presentation with the close. In other words, you cannot build their house without the building materials they first need to give you.

In sales, there is no template for when to close. The close is a byproduct of effective selling. How you present yourself, your belief in your product, your energy, and your tone all plays an essential part in separating yourself from everyone else. By meeting every question, objection, and technical requirement, your buyer will be confident enough to proceed with the sale. When you sell this way, closing is a formality. I cannot tell you how many people have stopped me halfway through a presentation over the years and said, "Let's just do it! I am ready to sign"; there was no actual close. In many cases, the prospect will close for you once you have gained their trust or when it is time to sign and get the check, there is an agreement with no resistance.

When you connect with the buyer, answer questions and objections, and lead the sale from behind, you have adequately met the buyer's needs emotionally, professionally, technically, and ethically.

Self-awareness is the driving factor to increasing emotional intelligence in sales and life. When you operate from an elevated level of self-awareness, you can objectively evaluate yourself while managing your emotions and the emotions of others in sales. As you become more self-aware, you produce an authentic version of yourself. You become centered and grounded, more confident in your abilities. You make better decisions, communicate more effectively, and build stronger relationships.

8 Steps to Grow Emotional Intelligence in Sales

1. How to Read Your Emotions and Others

Emotionally intelligent individuals recognize their power to influence the thoughts, words, and actions of others, all while staying in touch with their own emotions. They are acutely aware of how they feel. It's surprising to note that many people in sales lack this self-awareness, which impedes their ability to interpret their clients' emotions accurately. To understand others' emotions, one must first clearly understand their own. As we begin this change process, I encourage you to reflect on your feelings. Ask yourself, "How do I feel about what I'm experiencing now?" When standing in line at the grocery store or Starbucks, take a moment to observe others and try to sense their feelings quietly. Try to see the world from their perspective rather than your own.

When sitting with a prospect or assessing their needs over the phone, consider, "What are they going through right now?" Pay attention to their tone, get out of your head, and truly listen to what they say. We often perceive the world based on our experiences instead of trying to understand others. Perspective involves viewing the world from someone else's point of view; it means sitting in the person's seat opposite you. This shift allows you to ask what their life is like. How do they feel right now? What are they thinking? Moving from perception to perspective enhances self-awareness and refines emotional understanding. You'll begin to recognize what is happening "below the surface," so to speak. This will help you identify and interpret your emotions and your buyers.

2. Align Your Personality with The Buyer

Selling is fundamentally a game of personalities. You never want to make the prospect feel uncomfortable. You must know how your idiosyncrasies, actions, behaviors, physical presence, and selling style impact your buyer to avoid this.

When you are self-aware, you can quickly assess and align your perspective with the buyer's. Misinterpreting their emotions can create a disconnect in the buyer's mind, leading to distrust in the relationship. Self-awareness allows you to recognize important aspects of the buyer's behavior, enabling you to adapt and connect with them effectively. This understanding is only possible if you know how your personality impacts the buyer's experience. If the buyer feels uncomfortable, achieving a successful outcome becomes much more challenging. Your attitude, behavior, and selling style will influence the buyer's perception of you and ultimately affect the sale. By being self-aware of the buyer's personality, you can better understand and align your style and adjust your approach accordingly.

3. How You Introduce Yourself Matters

The first 90 seconds of your encounter with a buyer are pivotal; how you present yourself in these initial moments sets the tone for the respect they will have for you throughout the sales process. Your prospect is like a blank canvas, ready for you to make an impression. As a sales professional, you can shape how the prospect interacts with you. Your personality and body language all play a role. When you convey kindness, humility, and competence, showing genuine interest and learning more about them, you pave the way for a meaningful connection. I usually began my interactions by asking the prospect questions about themselves. Often, I will mention something I noticed about their property, home, or business. Allowing them to share their thoughts eases any fear or nervousness and lets them settle in before your presentation starts.

4. Being Authentic Translates to Trust

A World-Class Mindset recognizes the importance of relationships; establishing connections is a top priority. The goal is to develop confidence, safety, trust, and competence assurance. The strength of the connection is the strength of the sale. The most effective way to connect is by showing authenticity, vulnerability, and kindness. When you allow yourself to be vulnerable, your clients will feel comfortable enough to be vulnerable with you. People are more likely to make a purchase when they feel at ease. By mirroring authenticity and vulnerability, you create an environment where clients are safe and can think clearly. Your comfort level with yourself will reflect how comfortable your prospects feel with you.

5. Balance of Self-Confidence in Sales

At the beginning of a sale, your client assesses your confidence level while you present your product. They are trying to gauge whether you are in control of the situation. This assessment involves evaluating your character and how well you present yourself. The client will determine whether you come across as unsure or confident. This internal evaluation has little to do with the product itself; instead, it focuses on whether they like you and feel they can trust you.

Expressing self-confidence in sales is a delicate balance. It's important to understand that self-confidence is not the same as arrogance. It should not come across as imperious, pompous, or presumptuous. You must be mindful not to create an emotional disconnect with the prospect.

Many salespeople struggle with self-confidence and feel the need to present themselves as someone they are not when engaging with prospects. It's important to remember that this mindset can make it difficult for prospects to connect with you and feel comfortable moving forward. Buyers are looking for an authentic, confident expert who is trustworthy and comfortable in their skin. Lack of confidence is rarely related to your abilities and usually stems from your perceptions, which you have the power to change. Selling with confidence in sales involves two key elements. First, you must take control of the process. Prospects expect you to lead the conversation, demonstrate authority over your product, and showcase your expertise.

This includes having a comprehensive understanding of every technical aspect of your product, which will help address any doubts the prospect may have about your knowledge.

The second equally important element is expressing confidence. This transcends the product and creates a deeper connection with the prospect. It involves understanding what the prospect is seeking. How confident do you feel when sharing the benefits and features of your product? Prospects are always looking for ways to connect with you. You establish this connection by exhibiting contentment and happiness. Listening attentively, asking purposeful and substantive questions that demonstrate your understanding of their needs, maintaining eye contact, and showing that you genuinely enjoy being present and care about their concerns all contribute to building rapport. Self-confidence is an attitude that reflects your skills, abilities, and the product you sell. It means you trust and accept yourself while maintaining a sense of control. When you exhibit self-confidence, others can sense your positive perception of yourself. You communicate assertively and take charge of the information you share. By being grounded in who you are, your clients can feel the strength of your powerful, confident mindset. This confidence helps eliminate barriers of distrust, allowing them to feel safe and secure in your presence, which ultimately gives them the reassurance they need to move forward with you.

6. Empathy in Sales

Everyone has a story to tell. Empathy is the ability to understand, be aware of, and be sensitive to the thoughts and feelings of others. In sales, each person you meet has their own unique story. Understanding their feelings and thoughts enables you to navigate the sales process more effectively. When you form an emotional connection, you resonate with their experiences. However, if you don't develop this skill, you risk being on a different level of communication and may miss valuable opportunities, leading to ineffective communication and missed sales.

Selling is all about relational understanding. Understanding your customers' emotions gives you the power to guide the sales. Pay attention to something in the other person's environment that might have a story behind it. Use this observation to spark interest by asking a relevant question during your presentation. Listen carefully while they share their thoughts about your product and maintain good eye contact. A nod or a gesture can demonstrate empathy, concern, and genuine interest. The more you understand other people's emotions, intentions, motivations, and behaviors, the more effectively you can respond and interact with them during the sale. Remember, people buy based on emotions and justify their decisions with logic.

7. The Danger in Speaking Freely

At the beginning of every sale, if you have qualified the buyer well and the buyer has made time for you, the only variable in not getting the sale is you. A good percentage of the time, average salespeople do not get the sale because they share an opinion or a personal belief, state their values of how they feel, or some other issue they get carried away with, off the topic of the presentation. When you move away from the purpose of why you are there, you risk rubbing the buyer the wrong way. Stating your point of view is not why you are there unless asked by the buyer.

Every buyer has particular beliefs and social, political, and personal preferences. These are emotional landmines you do not want to step on or attempt to challenge in the slightest way. Your job is to agree when you can, and the rest of the time, stay neutral to any topic outside of why you are there. Stay in the safe zones by encouraging, complementing, and admiring things outside the presentation. You can also affirm the points the buyer is making by saying, "Yes, that is correct." "Exactly, I fully agree."

When your client is taking the chance to make a point, they risk being vulnerable in connecting with you, if possible, agree in some way. Even if their statement is inaccurate and does not apply to your product, let it go. If their statement does apply to the product and they have misunderstood you, be sensitive in sharing the correction, stating, "Yes! let me add to that by helping you see the product's full value." Any negative statements, unpleasant habits, or trying to undermine another product will cause the buyer to question your integrity and character.

8. The Power of Your Mindset Is in Your Eyes

William Shakespeare coined the phrase, "Eyes are the window of the soul." This phrase suggests that you can understand a person's emotions and feelings by looking into their eyes. Your eyes tell the story of who you are without asking any questions. Good eye contact is a sign of an adept communicator. It communicates that you have their undivided attention. Eyes are not merely a window but also a reflection of our mind and character. In sales, your eye contact is the connection that will either cause doubt or build confidence in the buyer's mind. Good eye contact is an essential non-verbal communication skill. People with a World-Class Mindset can emotionally support the sale by listening and expressing empathy, trust, confidence, kindness, and concern that can be seen and felt through their eyes. If these are your values, your eye contact, actions, and words will convey this to the buyer. However, one emotion expressed through your eyes is the king of the hill. It weaves and combines all these emotions. It's the deepest emotional fabric of your being and others. It is LOVE. Love is the most powerful emotion on the planet. It is a universal energy that connects us. Tapping into and living your life from it will free you from fear, failure, and other emotional chains that prevent emotional health. When others experience a gentle smile through eye contact as you proceed to share your product, you are content, calm, and have a peaceful demeanor. It is the most attractive trait you can share with the prospect. This attribute is the backdrop of your personality, presentation, and actions in sales.

It is a sense the buyer can feel and trust. Practicing a loving attitude and demeanor centers your thoughts and feelings on who you are. It resonates with the deepest authentic part of who others are. When you have a loving, kind presence, it decompresses the buyer's defense mechanism and helps them organize their emotions in connecting, feeling you are safe and trustworthy.

Summary
Mastering Emotional Intelligence in Sales

The fundamental principle of human psychology is that people tend to judge you based on your appearance first. They observe your body language, tone of voice, and how you present yourself physically and emotionally. Your appearance and how you carry yourself and communicate significantly influence how others perceive you. The quicker you can establish trust and demonstrate competence in a meeting, the more people will like and respect you. Your sales aptitude is scored by how many technical and emotional errors you make in the sales process. Your selling aptitude will dramatically increase when you elevate your sales awareness, make fewer mistakes, and can identify emotional landmines in yourself and the buyer. Emotional landmines are triggers that can set off negative emotions in the buyer, such as discussing a topic they are sensitive about (e.g. personal finances and values, not answering questions and objections with skill, feeling you're not prepared, etc.) Identifying and navigating these landmines is vital in sales, and it's a task that, with practice, you can master. This practice will not only improve your sales skills but also your confidence and emotional intelligence.

Honing this skill is not a simple task. It requires dedicated effort, including asking your prospects insightful questions and seeing situations, people, and opportunities from different perspectives. In this context, elite sales represent the highest level of sales proficiency, where you are not merely completing transactions but also building long-term relationships and deeply understanding the buyer's needs. This process involves both internal and external self-awareness in sales and a commitment to understanding and serving your clients. Enhancing and refining your emotional skills can be a game-changer in sales. Your mindset becomes a powerful asset. With experience and self-awareness, your instincts and intuition will guide you on what to say and how to say it, helping you evoke positive emotions in your buyer. Emotional intelligence is not a rigid template but a dynamic process that encourages creativity in finding common ground with the buyer.

As you develop self-awareness, a new perspective unfolds, transforming your emotions and enhancing your understanding of people. This heightened sensitivity becomes your most valuable tool in sales management. To truly master professional sales, you must practice and cultivate emotional intelligence.

In ending chapter 5 today, let us take a step back and see the big picture of this book. Remember, you are continuing to transform your mindset into a new space. It is new, the old you cannot enter this room. The only things that can enter and originate from this space are the principles in this book. You now have the Foundation of a **Growth Mindset**. 5 Steps to **Manage Resistance Fear and Failure.** 10 Steps to Strengthen Your **Mental Toughness,** 10 Steps in Maintaining a **World-Class Attitude** and 8 Principles to Increase Your **Emotional Intelligence.** As we continue to build and expand the values and principles in this book, stay in this room and start to embrace and apply the emotions and mindset you have learned.

Emotional Intelligence Questionnaire

Instructions: Rate your agreement with each statement below using the following scale: Be honest - this is about self-awareness, not perfection.

1 = Always (100%)-
2 = Often (about 75%)
3 = Sometimes (about 50%)
4 = Rarely (less than 25%)
5 = Never (0% of the time)

Section 1: Self-Awareness

1.	I can easily name the emotions I'm feeling at any given moment.	
2.	I understand how my mood affects my thoughts and behavior.	
3.	I reflect on my emotional responses after important events.	
4.	I recognize recurring emotional patterns in my life.	
5.	I am aware of how I come across when I'm under stress.	

Section 2: Self-Regulation

6.	I manage impulsive reactions in tense situations.	
7.	I stay calm and composed even when provoked.	
8.	I take responsibility for my emotional responses.	
9.	I make an effort to pause and think before responding emotionally.	
10.	I recover quickly after emotionally challenging events.	

Section 3: Motivation

11.	I pursue my goals even when I face repeated setbacks.
12.	I am driven by internal values more than external rewards.
13.	I remain optimistic even when progress is slow.
14.	I challenge myself to grow, even if success isn't guaranteed.
15.	I find purpose in the effort, not just the result.

Section 4: Empathy

16.	I can tell when someone is feeling upset, even if they don't say it.
17.	I make an effort to see situations from others' perspectives.
18.	I ask others how they feel rather than assuming.
19.	I try to understand someone's emotions before offering advice.
20.	I show genuine concern when others are struggling emotionally.

Section 5: Social Skills

21.	I communicate effectively with people from different backgrounds.
22.	I adapt my approach depending on who I'm interacting with.
23.	I resolve conflicts in a way that respects everyone involved.
24.	I make meaningful contributions to group conversations and decisions.
25.	I foster trust and rapport in both personal and professional relationships.

Score: (Total Possible Score (25-125)

> Add up your total score

Score 25–49 / Exceptional Emotional Intelligence - *You consistently demonstrate emotional mastery across all dimensions, awareness, regulation, empathy, motivation, and social finesse. You likely serve as an emotional anchor in your relationships and teams. You don't just react; you reflect, respond thoughtfully, and uplift those around you. Others likely seek your insight during moments of tension or uncertainty because you exude calm, clarity, and compassion.*

Score 50–74 / Strong EI Skills - *You possess solid emotional intelligence and apply it effectively in most situations. You're generally self-aware, emotionally steady, empathetic, and socially fluent, though you may notice the occasional stumble, perhaps under sustained stress or conflict. Still, you learn quickly from emotional experiences and are receptive to feedback.*

Score 75–99 / Moderate EI - *You show growing self-awareness and the capacity to empathize and regulate, but the expression of these abilities might be inconsistent. Specific triggers may derail your emotional clarity, or social dynamics might feel overwhelming at times. You're likely working to understand your patterns and seeking practical strategies for more consistency.*

Score 100–125 / Emerging EI Skills - *This score suggests emotional intelligence may be underdeveloped, unrecognized, or hidden behind internal or external challenges. It may feel difficult to name feelings, empathize deeply, or respond thoughtfully in stressful moments but this doesn't mean those capacities don't exist. They're just waiting to be cultivated with awareness, practice, and support.*

CHAPTER 6
WORLD-CLASS RESPONSIBILITY
THE ARCHITECTURE OF ACCOUNTABILITY THAT SHAPES PERFORMANCE

This attribute is instrumental in the success of a World-Class Mindset, the action of world-class responsibility! Responsibility is one of the main pillars necessary for producing a highly effective life. Responsibility is accepting what is required and carrying out the task to the best of your ability.

Where average responsibility ends and begins at task completion, world-class responsibility extends deeper; it monitors emotional integrity, recalibrates misalignment, and sustains behavioral congruence even when external visibility is absent. Responsibility at this level rejects emotional outsourcing (*"They made me feel," "This ruined my energy," "I can't do my best until..."*). It replaces reactivity with reflection. It pauses the urge to defend and replaces it with the drive to refine.

It can't go unnoticed because it determines your character and competence in business and personal life. It's action-driven and is a big part of a world-class attitude. Being trustworthy, accountable, dependable, and entirely in control of what you think, say, and do gives you the freedom to grow to your full potential. Responsibility is infused into all aspects of our lives.

What drives responsibility the most is emotional intelligence. Again, emotional intelligence is your ability to identify and understand your and other people's emotions. Emotional maturity is accountability for your actions, behaviors, thoughts, and feelings. It demonstrates self-awareness and the belief that we can change and do better. It is the ability to deliver what you are responsible for in an appropriate way based on the situation and people involved. However, one of life's most significant obstacles to change and growth is being unable to see the initial problem or unwilling to see the issue. Suppose your mindset is in defense mode. "I don't believe that it's my fault." "There is nothing I can do about it." "Nobody answered. I called and called, so I didn't sell anything this week." You are in the cycle of being a victim, always looking outside of yourself when things go wrong.

People who struggle to accept responsibility find it easier to blame others or their circumstances than to be accountable. They live in denial and ignore the truth of the situation. This mindset is costly because it's self-defeating and doesn't align with your expected actions. Every action and reaction move the barometer of responsibility in some way. Everything you do runs through the heart of it, and that is why it plays such an essential role in your character. When your character is a liability to others and affects their ability to see you as solid and reliable, you create self-inflicted resistance, disabling your ability to succeed.

So, the question is, why? Why is taking responsibility so hard for people to manage? What causes people to neglect responsibility? People avoid responsibility for many reasons: Laziness, fear of failure, shame, pride, painful past experiences, or feeling overwhelmed by the enormity of a problem or situation. It's an attitude that exposes vulnerability because it allows everyone to see how they think and operate.

Your emotional health directly relates to your ability to be responsible for your job and others around you. Suppose you find yourself blaming others, lacking interest, missing deadlines, avoiding challenges or risks, regularly complaining, not meeting your production goals, and making excuses. In that case, you are in a mindset of irresponsibility! This must change to develop a World-Class Mindset. So how do we achieve this?

How to Build a Mindset of Responsibility

The answer is – in the first five chapters and throughout this book.

Chapter 1: *Evaluate Your Mindset*, examined the differences between fixed and growth mindsets. Individuals with a growth mindset refrain from labeling or judging themselves and persist even in the face of distress. They are open to taking risks and confronting challenges, and their ability to keep moving forward despite obstacles showcases their resilience and strength. Furthermore, they recognize the importance of pushing their limits and maintaining effort when faced with setbacks.

Chapter 2: We discussed the concepts of *Resistance, Fear, and Failure*. I emphasized that you would encounter resistance whenever you take a principled stand, whether in the face of adversity or while pursuing something meaningful. The key to embracing responsibility is to trust yourself and not suppress your emotions. Although it may seem daunting, the best approach is to allow resistance to flow through you. It never truly disappears; it is a part of human nature. However, by understanding resistance, you can gain the power to overcome it. Avoiding responsibility will only deepen your emotional resistance.

Chapter 3: *Mental Toughness*, we explored your daily mental challenges. Your primary opponent is resistance, shaped by your responses to various external pressures, such as your job, relationships, income, and opportunities. Life is inherently challenging and generates a natural force of resistance that you must navigate.

Chapter 4: *World-Class Attitude*, I said that when you are self-aware, you grow stronger by managing and developing positive self-belief habits. This attitude is not hindered by self-sabotaging thoughts that weigh on your performance. As you create a shield of emotional strength, your personality, actions, and beliefs change as you take on this mindset.

Chapter 5: We examined the importance of *Emotional Intelligence* (EI) as a vital component in managing ourselves and others. EI serves as the thinker, planner, strategist, diplomat, and psychologist within the metaphorical castle where battles are fought, and outcomes are determined. Your leadership success is closely tied to your ability to navigate the various attitudes, challenges, and stresses you encounter.

Throughout this book, we have focused on the concept of responsibility, which has been the underlying theme in all the chapters.

There is a direct correlation between responsibility and success in any human endeavor; the depth of responsibility that is grounded in you equals the opportunities you will produce in your life. It takes courage to raise the bar of responsibility because it requires looking into the mirror and flushing out all false perceptions and judgments you've had about yourself and others.

It's entering the dungeons of who we are and turning the light on. In many cases, we hide by avoiding the things we must face. But the more authentically you live, the more power you gain to face any issue. It takes emotionally strong people to look honestly at their circumstances and to do the right thing. It's a journey that will continually test your emotional strength if you allow yourself to stay on the path and develop this habit of responsibility.

> *"The man who blames others has a long way to go. The man who blames himself is halfway there. The man who blames no one is already there"* - Chinese Proverb

10 Steps to Maintain and Manage Responsibility!

1. I Am Responsible

Avoiding responsibility affects not only your mindset but also the reality of the situation. By acknowledging "I am responsible," you lay the foundation for empowerment. Accepting the consequences and stating "I am responsible," demonstrates your accountability. By taking the heat and saying, "I am responsible," you show your commitment to growth and inspire others with your determination.

2. How Others View Your Actions

Taking responsibility for your mistakes might seem like it could reflect poorly on you, but the reality is quite the opposite. It demonstrates strength and integrity, qualities that people admire. Acknowledging your errors shows humility, honesty, and a refusal to make excuses. In fact, it can even lead others to look up to you.

3. Integrity Leads Responsibility

Honor your commitments, avoid procrastination, and be trustworthy and accountable. Treat others fairly and be mindful of your words and actions. These qualities are highly respected in sales, the world, and your personal life.

4. Clearly Define Your Responsibilities

It's important to recognize that you are not accountable for the actions, feelings, or words of others. Your responsibility lies in how you respond to their behavior. Remember that you are entirely responsible for your thoughts and actions; it can be beneficial to remind yourself of this when needed.

5. Responsibility Empowers

Taking responsibility empowers individuals. I have encountered many intelligent people who excel in various areas of life yet struggle to say "I'm sorry" or admit when they are wrong. However, when someone acknowledges their mistakes, takes accountability for letting others down, or owns up to unfinished tasks, they naturally emerge as a leader within the group. People tend to view them as leaders. True leaders are rare and often rise to the top.

6. Trust Yourself Under Pressure

When faced with the burden or pressure of a situation you are responsible for, your decision-making, mental strength, and character will come to the forefront. Learn to trust yourself and continue pushing through any resistance you may encounter. Remember, each time you do, you strengthen your mindset and inspire others with your determination.

7. Top Producers Are Proactive

Highly skilled salespeople take ownership of their standards. This mindset influences every aspect of their identity and approach to selling. The company hired you to sell and maintain a certain level of production. You are responsible for creating a marketing and sales system to achieve these goals.

8. Responsibility Replenishes Your Power

People who perform at an elite level will be the first to tell you they are not perfect and that mistakes are okay. They understand that taking responsibility is not a burden but a source of empowerment. It replenishes your power when you make a mistake, giving you a sense of control and confidence.

9. Keep Moving Forward

Don't let failure strip you of your sense of responsibility, tough times affect everyone. Instead of seeing yourself as a victim who is helpless and powerless, take ownership of the situation. Do what is necessary to keep moving forward.

10. Prelude to Success

The more you are willing to take responsibility, the more confidence and personal power you gain, which helps to develop your character. Responsibility is key to success; without it in your work, personal life, and self, you cannot develop a World-Class Mindset.

> *Winston Churchill said it plays a big part in the scale of your success.*
>
> *He said- The price of greatness is – Responsibility!*

Open a New Room You Have Never Entered

At the end of chapter 6 today, you are well on your way to learning and managing the mindset and principles of highly successful people. Remember, you are continuing to transform your mindset into a new space. It is new, the old, you cannot enter this room. The only things that can enter and originate from this space are the principles in this book. You now have the foundation of a **Growth Mindset**. 5 steps to manage **Resistance, Fear, and Failure.**

10 steps to strengthen your **Mental Toughness,** 10 steps in maintaining a **World-Class Attitude,** and 8 principles to increase your **Emotional Intelligence.** 10 principles of **World-Class Responsibility.** As we continue to build and expand the values and principles in this book, stay in this room and continue to embrace and apply what you have learned.

Sales Responsibility Questionnaire

Instructions: Rate your agreement with each statement below using the following scale: Be honest—this is about self-awareness, not perfection.

1 = Always (100%)
2 = Often (about 75%)
3 = Sometimes (about 50%)
4 = Rarely (less than 25%)
5 = Never (0% of the time)

Section 1: Personal Accountability

1.	I take full ownership of both my sales wins and losses.	
2.	I avoid blaming others for missed sales or missteps.	
3.	I take ownership of fixing mistakes, even if they weren't my fault.	
4.	I finish what I start, even when enthusiasm fades.	
5.	I handle rejection constructively without deflecting blame.	

Section 2: Client Commitment & Trust

6.	I keep commitments made to customers, regardless of their size or scope.	
7.	I clarify misunderstandings before they escalate.	
8.	I communicate delays or changes with transparency.	
9.	I disclose limitations or downsides of my product honestly.	
10.	I prioritize long-term relationships over quick wins.	

Section 3: Initiative & Self-Development

11.	I proactively follow up with prospects without being prompted.	
12.	I take initiative to improve my product or industry knowledge.	
13.	I regularly set personal targets beyond company goals.	
14.	I actively seek feedback from customers or managers.	
15.	I regularly review my performance and adjust accordingly.	

Section 4: Operational Integrity

16.	I meet deadlines for submitting production, proposals, or updates.	
17.	I maintain accurate and up-to-date CRM records.	
18.	I stay organized with my sales pipeline and tasks.	
19.	I respond promptly to emails, calls, or inquiries.	
20.	I respect the client's time by being punctual and prepared.	

Section 5: Ethics & Collaboration

21.	I address ethical concerns head-on rather than ignore them.	
22.	I ensure a seamless handoff between sales and service.	
23.	I escalate client issues responsibly when needed.	
24.	I consistently research my clients' needs before contacting them.	
25.	I remain accountable even when a deal goes south.	

Scoring: (Total Possible Score: 25–125)

Add up your total score	

Score 25–50 / Exemplary Responsibility - *You're the gold standard. Your proactive mindset builds trust and drives consistent success. You're dependable and often a role model. Now, the challenge is staying sharp and empowering others.*

Score 51–75 / Reliable, With Room to Sharpen - *Strong baseline behaviors, but some habits may lack consistency. Target your "4s" and "5s" to solidify your edge. Tightening up habits and leaning into discomfort will elevate you further.*

Score 76–100 / Variable Accountability *-Your approach is situational. Consider whether distraction, lack of structure, or discomfort drives avoidance. Raising self-awareness is the first lever for more consistent action.*

Score 101–115 / In Need of Ownership Shift - *There may be patterns of avoidance, denial, or reactive behavior. You may deflect or retreat from hard conversations, deadlines, or outcomes. Growth starts with confronting discomfort honestly.*

Score 116–125 / Urgent Reset Needed - *This may indicate chronic avoidance or erosion of credibility. You may be disengaged, disconnected, or overwhelmed. Responsibility can be rebuilt, but it starts with brutal honesty and safe accountability. It's a signal for guided change.*

CHAPTER 7
THE POWER OF NOW
THE ART OF RELENTLESS PRESENCE

The Power of NOW is the disciplined practice of anchoring identity, awareness, and action into the present moment—*without distortion from past patterns or projection into imagined futures*. It's not passive mindfulness, it's strategic presence.

Most people live reactively in time, haunted by past failures, preoccupied with uncertain outcomes, or hijacked by emotional residue. But elite performers understand that power only exists in NOW: the moment where choice lives, where alignment is possible, and where identity is expressed through decision.

Achieving high-performance productivity doesn't just occur; it requires purposeful and deliberate action that thrives in the present moment. Many people in sales struggle because their mindset lacks focus. Their attention is scattered across various distractions. They often replay past mistakes in their minds, worry about future ambitions, or become sidetracked by personal issues that demand their attention.

Our mental energy is depleted by not fully experiencing our lives in the present moment. Most of our time is spent outside of the NOW. The truth is that our lives are constantly occurring in the NOW. Thoughts about the past and future can prevent us from being present. Fear is our most mismanaged emotion, as it often stems from worries about the future. When we live outside of the NOW, we risk manifesting outcomes we don't want, such as losing income, procrastinating, feeling frustrated or stressed, and failing to meet family obligations. Our habits shape our mindset, and when we dwell on the past or obsess over the future, we create a cycle of habits that undermines our ability to succeed.

Embracing the present moment opens the door to empowerment and freedom. It allows you to fully engage with your experiences, making you feel alive, excited, and motivated. By staying present, you confront each moment directly, whether it's a joyful occasion or a challenging situation. Cultivating this habit will ultimately lead to greater success, happiness, and fulfillment. Adopting a World-Class Mindset means shifting your focus outward and committing to decisive actions. "I will make 50 calls today," "I will practice my script," and "I need to prepare for my upcoming meeting." Every thought and effort must zero in on solutions and active engagement during work hours. Prioritize the sales process, focus on the actions, not just the outcomes. Embrace the present moment, your "NOW", and own it as your action zone.

The key is to focus on what you can control: your effort! Your performance and income will improve when you concentrate on consistent daily effort. When fully engaged in the "power zone of NOW," you activate your potential at its highest capacity and operate at your peak productivity. But how can you maintain this focus consistently?

By Moving NOW! Into the power of the HOUR! Your power lives in every moment of this hour! Stay as productive as possible in this hour! Move throughout your workday in focused hour segments with no interference. Choose specific hours and dedicate them to working in the power of the hour. By operating in the power of the hour, you take control of your attention, sharpen your focus, and elevate your productivity to impressive levels. Many top producers adopt this approach to work efficiently every hour.

Learn to schedule and manage your time with yourself as you would with any other appointment each day. When was the last time you truly worked for a full 60 minutes in an hour? By implementing and embracing the concept of "NOW" within the "power of the hour," you can gain a clearer awareness of the actual hours you work each week and concentrate your efforts on managing your time effectively. You might be surprised to discover that you are not working as many focused hours as you think. The more you focus and remain in your "power zone of NOW," the stronger your mindset will become. Staying present helps neutralize concerns about the past and worries about the future. While it doesn't eliminate the problems or challenges you face daily, it will empower you to deal with them more effectively.

3 Steps in Managing Your Power Zone of NOW

1. Managing NOW

What interferes with your ability to stay focused in your power zone of NOW? Is anger, worry, self-doubt, fear, disappointment, or the influence of others consuming your time? These are emotional distractions that can lead you away from the present moment. They can be fleeting, a sudden impulse to act, leading us into certain emotions, without realizing they control us. If they persist, they can become a mood or attitude, shaping our thought process.

2. Your Power Zone

Become self-aware when your emotions start to control you. It's important to understand how your feelings respond to adverse events. People skilled in self-awareness can manage their thoughts, emotions, and attitudes as they come and manage them accordingly. They are sensitive to how these moods can bind and hijack their mindset outside their power zone. Do you need to be right all the time? Do you need to look good? Are you easily insulted? Are you in denial, driven by ego, arrogant, pretentious, or wasting time? These attitudes bind and move you away from staying centered in your power zone of NOW. - Self-awareness is the beginning of breaking free from the emotions that drive you. You will begin to realize that your negative thoughts are pointless. When you learn to stay in the moment of NOW – accepting – "What is," you won't need to attach to negative emotions or take things personally.

3. Your Emotions

People who live in the present are finely tuned to their emotions and attitudes. We all have unpleasant feelings, such as being criticized or challenged and experiencing disappointment or rejection. We also have emotions we enjoy, exhilaration, joy, contentment, or a sense of accomplishment. Good or bad, allowing yourself to experience your feelings entirely is the point. The silver lining in living your emotions is they bring a vivid sense of being alive that is not possible without them. The more you experience, the more you learn. If you ignore your emotions, you will not know what needs to change. You will be unable to live a fully authentic life. Experiencing our feelings is an essential building block in developing who we are.

Children are the best example of embracing their emotions while living in the moment. They are fully present whether they are experiencing curiosity, wonder, love, joy, or sadness. They make life simple. It is an experience! Neither the past nor the future can interfere with their actions. You are living in the power zone of NOW when you fully experience your emotions without condemning, labeling, or needing to respond. Your ability to execute effectively in sales depends on your emotional freedom to stay present. A World-Class Mindset's best friend is "NOW."

Power of NOW Questionnaire

Instructions: Rate your agreement with each statement below using the following scale: Be honest—this is about self-awareness, not perfection.

1 = Always (100%)
2 = Often (about 75%)
3 = Sometimes (about 50%)
4 = Rarely (less than 25%)
5 = Never (0% of the time)

Section 1: Action & Urgency

1.	I follow up with leads within hours, not days.	
2.	I treat each conversation as if it may be the turning point in the deal.	
3.	I rarely procrastinate on high-impact sales actions.	
4.	I respond to client inquiries quickly, even if it's just to acknowledge them.	
5.	I proactively suggest the next steps at the moment rather than waiting to "circle back."	

Section 2: Presence & Focus

6.	Stay fully engaged during client conversations without multitasking.	
7.	I actively listen instead of waiting to speak.	
8.	I am aware of my tone, pacing, and nonverbal cues in calls and meetings.	
9.	I give my full attention to one sales opportunity at a time.	
10.	I notice and adjust when a prospect's mood or energy shifts.	

Section 3: Mental Clarity & Intentionality

11.	I pursue my goals even when I face repeated setbacks.
12.	I am driven by internal values more than external rewards.
13.	I remain optimistic even when progress is slow.
14.	I challenge myself to grow, even if success isn't guaranteed.
15.	I find purpose in the effort, not just the result.

Section 4: Momentum & Follow-Through

16.	I move a deal forward within 24 hours of every significant conversation.
17.	I prepare agendas in advance to drive productive meetings.
18.	I never let discomfort delay an important outreach.
19.	I use time blocks or similar techniques to maintain productive flow.
20.	I document and act on follow-ups immediately after meetings.

Section 5: Time Mastery & Ownership

21.	I limit distractions and protect "deep work" time.
22.	I complete daily sales priorities without rollover.
23.	I front-load my schedule to make space for the unexpected.
24.	I treat urgency as a habit, not a reaction.
25.	I choose NOW over perfect starting before I feel 100% ready.

Scoring: (Total Possible Score: 25–125)

Add up your total score	

Score 25–50 / NOW-Led Performer - *You're decisively present and action-oriented. Your urgency inspires results and confidence. You don't waste a second. Whether it's seizing momentum in a live*

call, responding decisively to objections, or capitalizing on micro-opportunities between meetings, you live in the moment with intention. You lead with presence, not pressure, balancing urgency with composure. Clients feel your attentiveness. Colleagues rely on your follow-through. You're not just fast; you're aware, engaged, and adaptive in real-time.

Score 51–75 / Consistently Timely with Pockets of Delay - *You demonstrate a strong baseline of urgency and responsiveness. You're capable of stepping up when it matters. However, you may unconsciously triage specific actions, letting tasks that feel less urgent, emotionally taxing, or less visible drift. Some delays may stem from over-perfectionism, emotional resistance (e.g., fear of rejection or negative feedback), or lack of clarity on what's "worth" acting on now.*

Score 76–100 / Intermittent Presence and Proactivity - *You're capable. You show up. But not always all in. Your sales presence has flashes of brilliance—when focus, energy, and urgency align, but those flashes are sporadic. At other times, you may feel distracted, mentally elsewhere during calls, or stuck overanalyzing instead of taking action. Tasks slip through the cracks not because you don't care but because your attention is fragmented or your trigger to act is inconsistently engaged. You're chasing the moment, not steering it.*

Score 101–115 / Passive or Hesitant Engagement - *You're likely insightful, thoughtful, and capable, but your timing is off. You often recognize what needs to be done... and then hesitate. The moment to act drifts past. It's not a matter of ignorance; it's the lag between recognition and execution. This hesitation may stem from perfectionism, fear of being judged, unclear priorities, or even mental fatigue from over-processing. It's a form of self-protection disguised as "waiting for the right time."*

Score 116–125 / Urgency Vacuum - *In this state, time passes, but momentum doesn't follow. You might know what needs to happen, yet feel paralyzed, burnt out, or indifferent. Action is delayed not because you lack skill but because focus feels fractured and motivation is drained. Tasks that once felt energizing now seem heavy. You may find yourself reacting to the day instead of driving it, stuck in loops of avoidance, overthinking, or just emotional fatigue.*

CHAPTER 8
AUTHENTIC ENTHUSIASM
EXPRESSING BELIEF, NOT PERFORMING EMOTION

In a high-performance culture, false enthusiasm is everywhere. Overcompensation. Conditional optimism. Energetic inflation for performance's sake. But authentic enthusiasm isn't a tactic; it's emotional truth in motion.

Unlike synthetic enthusiasm, which is often borrowed from results, applause, or external momentum, authentic enthusiasm is authored from the inside out. It's how intensity speaks when it's sourced from truth, not performance.

Enthusiasm is the foundation upon which all other positive emotions are built. It is the most powerful tool in your sales arsenal. To illustrate its strength, I like to use the metaphor of dark matter, which is believed to hold planets in space. Although scientists cannot explain dark matter, it exists and invisibly secures all the stars and planets in their proper positions. Similarly, enthusiasm serves as the invisible force that keeps the sales process in place. Although it cannot be seen and doesn't need to be explicitly discussed, it serves as a powerful, invisible energy of influence in sales.

When you create an environment of enthusiasm, you are physically changing the metabolic system of your prospect. We can feel enthusiasm when it is around us. We see it used most effectively in sports, coaching, and business. At its core, enthusiasm embodies a deep-seated belief in our identity, who we are, what we do, and what we want to achieve in life.

Much like a magnifying glass that harnesses the power of light enough to burn a piece of paper, enthusiasm has the same effect. It takes someone's energy and excitement for life and organizes it into a coherent stream of productivity. Enthusiasm not only moves people to action but also draws people to you. Everyone is moved by it. It is a positive energy that moves people closer to a "Yes" than a "No," in sales.

Enthusiasm is a powerful force that drives commitment and effort, enabling individuals to achieve their goals more quickly. It triggers a range of positive emotions, including motivation, persistence, determination, diligence, and tenacity. You can recognize whether you possess enthusiasm by observing how it manifests in your being, your words, and your actions. Enthusiasm is grounded in integrity; when you embrace it, you'll find yourself attending more appointments, arriving on time, and delivering presentations with the right energy and intensity. However, it's important to note that enthusiasm cannot be contrived, it must be genuine. So, how can you discover what sparks authentic enthusiasm within you?

Understanding Your Role as A Communicator

First, you need to understand your role as a communicator. Enthusiasm is infectious when it comes to sales. The client comes alive when you genuinely share your passion for your product and are excited about what it can do for your prospect. They see and feel it, too. Alternatively, they can feel a flat, uninspired presentation is a death spiral. What does it take for you to be inspired?

Enthusiasm is the continuity that maintains the energy in the sale. Your voice and tone determine whether they believe what you are saying. Your enthusiasm lifts the words off the brochure and inspires your prospect as you share.

Let's compare two movies. I'll use *Gladiator* and *Dumb and Dumber*. The ticket price is the same for both films. Which one left you feeling inspired and emotionally moved? Which one did you leave uplifted, saying, "That was a great movie." Like watching a great film, you are the main character who embodies these attributes in sales. You have the prospect's full attention. They are listening intently to what you are presenting. They are involved in your story. Your personality and passion bring your product alive. This is what moves the buyer to say, let's do it! Sign me up! However, enthusiasm in sales is a delicate balance.

The question is, how do you deliver the appropriate amount of enthusiasm? It is an inner strength of joy, passion, and desire to be the best at what you do and for your client. It comes naturally when you are authentic about presenting yourself and the product. Enthusiasm is the magnet of energy the buyer feels and connects with. To be an elite in sales, you must have authentic enthusiasm!

3 Steps to Grow Authentic Enthusiasm

1. It is Not a Skill You Learn.

Discovering your true potential requires a deep understanding of your beliefs, attitudes, and purpose. When you define your mission statement and clarify your goals, you'll ignite a powerful enthusiasm for executing your plan and pursuing your dreams.

2. Letting Go of What Doesn't Work

When you let go of emotional baggage and develop self-awareness, you assert your freedom. Embrace your emotions with confidence, and you will unlock a powerful sense of enthusiasm that can drive your life forward.

3. Action Based Mindset

Enthusiasm is a powerful, action-oriented mindset. Actively pursue knowledge and strategies for success, and you will unlock an abundance of energy and enthusiasm within yourself.

Open a New Room You Have Never Entered

You now have the foundation of a **Growth Mindset**. 5 steps to manage **Resistance, Fear, and Failure.** 10 steps to strengthen your **Mental Toughness,** 10 steps in maintaining a **World-Class Attitude,** and 8 principles to increase your **Emotional Intelligence.** 10 principles of **World-Class Responsibility.** 3 steps to harness the **The Power of NOW,** and 3 steps to grow **Authentic Enthusiasm.**

As you conclude this chapter, remember that you're on a transformative journey, evolving your mindset to embrace a new and empowering perspective. Let go of your old thought patterns that cannot enter this room. Only the empowering principles from this book can thrive in this space. By allowing these principles to take hold in your mindset, you will set yourself on a successful path to effectively applying them in your sales strategy.

Authentic Enthusiasm Questionnaire

Instructions: Rate your agreement with each statement below using the following scale: Be honest—this is about self-awareness, not perfection.

1 = Always (100%)
2 = Often (about 75%)
3 = Sometimes (about 50%)
4 = Rarely (less than 25%)
5 = Never (0% of the time)

Section 1: Inner Drive & Passion

1.	I genuinely enjoy helping customers solve their problems.	
2.	I feel energized before (not just after) client conversations.	
3.	I speak about my product or service with personal conviction.	
4.	I can articulate why I believe in what I sell—beyond the script.	
5.	I stay motivated even when deals stagnate or get delayed.	

Section 2: Expressiveness & Positivity

6.	My tone and facial expressions reflect real excitement.	
7.	I bring contagious energy into my sales conversations.	
8.	I know how to light up when talking about customer wins.	
9.	I naturally use stories and analogies that show I care.	
10.	My enthusiasm feels intuitive, not forced or rehearsed.	

Section 3: Curiosity & Engagement

11.	I ask questions with sincere curiosity, not just obligation.
12.	I often find myself interested in the prospect's world or industry.
13.	I actively listen for emotional cues, not just technical needs.
14.	I find it easy to be present and dial in on discovery calls.
15.	My responses sound thoughtful rather than transactional.

Section 4: Integrity & Belief

16.	I can say, "This might not be the right fit," without losing momentum.
17.	My enthusiasm doesn't waver when I tell hard truths.
18.	I advocate for the customer, even if it challenges the status quo.
19.	I never pretend to be excited; I either reconnect or stay quiet.
20.	I'd stand by my solution even if there were no commissions involved.

Section 5: Resilience & Emotional Energy

21.	I can reset quickly after a tough conversation.
22.	I rarely fake excitement—I recharge instead.
23.	I celebrate small wins internally (not just externally).
24.	I know how to reconnect with my "why" in down cycles.
25.	I regularly take care of my mental and emotional energy.

Scoring: (Total Possible Score: 25–125)

Add up your total score	

Score 25–50 / Authentic Flame - *You're not "selling"; you're translating belief into action. Customers can feel your alignment: your words match your intention, your energy is grounded in service, and your conviction comes from experience, not ego. You speak from clarity, not performance. And when you get excited, it's not theater; it's truth rising to the surface. You don't need to fake enthusiasm because you've connected your product to a greater purpose.*

Score 51–75 / Mostly Engaged, Occasionally Flat – *You show up. You say the right things. You're consistent, respectful, and reliable. But under the surface, something might be missing: a spark, an edge, or a genuine emotional charge. Enthusiasm becomes a gear you switch into rather than a frequency you live in. When the energy dips, it doesn't crash; it just goes dull. It's not burnout; it's disconnection. The fix isn't about skill; it's about reigniting alignment.*

Score 76–100 / Performing Without Connecting – *This is like watching a talented actor recite lines perfectly but without emotional impact. It's not a failure of skill; it's a disconnection from meaning. You're sharp. You know the material. You've got the language, the timing, and the delivery. But your enthusiasm feels manufactured. What's missing isn't effort; it's emotional access. At this level, enthusiasm becomes performance rather than presence. Conversations lack texture, and your voice lacks the conviction that moves people not just to buy but to believe. What you're missing isn't charisma; it's connection to purpose. It requires a reset in how you engage emotionally with the story you're telling.*

Score 101–115 / Emotionally Disengaged or Disconnected - *Sales may feel robotic. You may be feeling burned out, bored, or uncertain about what you believe in anymore. This disengagement could stem from unresolved burnout, a growing disconnect between your values and your message, or emotional fatigue from years of masking effort with enthusiasm. You may wonder: Is this* *really it? Do I still believe in what I'm doing?* If unaddressed, this stage can quietly drain your confidence, creativity, and credibility. But if acknowledged, it can become the birthplace of your most aligned and sustainable form of leadership, not louder energy, but a more authentic expression.

Score 116–125 / Enthusiasm Sales Crisis - When someone's in an enthusiasm crisis, it isn't about competence; it's about disconnection, it's about numbness. You may find yourself going through the motions, giving the pitch, attending the meetings, and logging the calls, but it feels hollow. There's a quiet fatigue beneath the surface. It doesn't mean you've failed. It means you've lost the emotional **WHY,** that reason beyond revenue. This kind of crisis often stems from a misalignment between your values and your message, your strengths and your tasks, or your effort and your recognition. But the crisis also signals a threshold. It's time to find a new layer of truth, purpose, and practice. Let's breathe life into this with honesty, strategy, and emotional clarity.

CHAPTER 9
THE DEATH STARS OF OUR EMOTIONS - THE 3 R'S
EMOTIONAL SABOTEURS OF PERFORMANCE

Three powerful emotions will profoundly restrict your success. These are the cataclysmic supernovas of our negative emotions. To use a Star Wars analogy, this would be the death star that circles your world. Anything weak near its gravitational force will suck you in as a victim and sideline your ability for years, some a lifetime. It could be your marriage, business, or what prevents you from succeeding. These negative emotions are far-reaching and have the potential to do the most damage in building a World-Class Mindset. We could spend hours discussing these emotions and even days in therapy examining their impact on people's lives. However, my goal today is to raise your awareness about the power of these emotional traps, which can hinder your development in life and sales.

They're the 3 R's: **Resentment, Resistance, and Revenge** are not just emotions, they're deeply embedded psychological loops that quietly hijack your energy, distort your judgment, and disrupt your identity alignment. Most people don't realize that these emotional patterns operate beneath their awareness, like malware in the operating system of behavior. Together, these emotions become emotional handcuffs disguised as protection but functioning as suppression. You can't lead from resentment. You can't grow from revenge. You can't execute with resistance. These emotions don't just cost clarity, they cost identity.

The First "R": Resentment

Of all the futile and destructive emotions humans are prey to, the most universal is the mindset of resentment. This emotion thrives on the belief that we have been wronged, causing us to fixate on perceived injustices. Whether it's feeling entitled to something we didn't receive or watching someone else attain what we feel they didn't earn, resentment takes root. We envy those who appear to have more: be it wealth, success, or even happiness. This can extend to colleagues, friends, spouses, and even our children. Psychologists have observed that most resentful people blame their parents for their inability to succeed. They believe that the reason they have failed is not because they lack the talent, energy, or determination to succeed but because factors beyond their control are unjustly stacked against them. I am not to blame. I have an excuse why I am not capable.

Psychologists report that these destructive emotions have more to do with the inner need to justify the injustice in our lives rather than managing our circumstances. Undoubtedly, we all have felt resentment, provoking a cascade of emotions like anger, disappointment, and bitterness. These emotions are frequently triggered by common situations we all face, dealing with people who refuse to consider other viewpoints, feeling exploited, being belittled, not being heard, or experiencing victimization in any form. Resentment, in its various forms, can be a powerful emotion. If you're dealing with resentment, it's important to recognize the signs such as recurring anger triggered by specific thoughts or feelings of regret, not being acknowledged or respected. Whether it's a situation where you're trying to avoid conflict, or when your boss or friend makes an unflattering remark about you or your style, understanding these triggers is the first step to taking control of your emotional well-being.

However, resentment can be temporary, only needing to hear a sincere apology, or it can become a persistent emotion determining how we operate through life. Regardless of whether the source of resentment is people, circumstances, or family, there is only one way to escape this negative death star that wants to dwarf your power to succeed: by strengthening your mindset. Resentful emotions are powerful because they can keep our minds captive, giving us a false sense of control in expressing ourselves.

Our anger and resentment often stem from our expectations about how things "should be," instead of accepting "what is." This struggle to embrace reality distorts our perspective: when something occurs, we might think, "That's unfair; it should have gone differently. I don't deserve this." In these moments, we focus on our hurt and anger, contemplating revenge against those who wronged us. However, this mindset holds us back. We should instead ask, "What steps can I take to address this issue or prevent it from recurring?"

When we allow ourselves to be ruled by anger or resentment, we hand over our emotional power to others, diminishing our strength and hindering our ability to navigate the situation effectively. Embracing acceptance empowers us to take control and find constructive solutions that promote healing and growth.

Stealth Resentment

There exists a subtle yet pervasive form of resentment that can be particularly challenging to identify, I call it, stealth resentment. You may consider yourself free from feelings of resentment, and that may indeed be accurate. However, this insidious emotion has the remarkable ability to seep into our consciousness and become embedded in our thought processes and behaviors without our conscious realization. It operates quietly, influencing our interactions and decisions, often in ways we are not even aware of.

When an insult or an unjust situation arises, and we start to feel resentful, it's possible to catch ourselves and manage these emotions. But do you ever talk about things you want to change in others, wishing things were different in your work environment? Do you ever feel powerless over people, places, or situations you want to change? If we stay in this mindset too long, it can become ingrained in our thinking.

Stealth resentment quietly manifests itself, keeping our minds in an altered state of reality. We find ourselves wishing we could change things instead of accepting "what is." Recognizing that we are powerless over what others say or do helps solidify our mindset, allowing us to focus on and produce results in the areas that matter most to us. In the context of sales, you might believe you are free from resentment. However, if you find yourself trying to dominate, control, or manipulate others to conform to your way of thinking, you are opening the door to resentment.

People don't buy from those who try to change them. They buy from those who listen and understand, allowing them to shape the sale according to their interests. When you lead from behind, you adopt a mindset of acceptance, being fully present and prepared to address any obstacles that may arise while meeting your client's needs.

When you stay centered in the strength of joy, peace, gratitude, trust, and forgiveness these emotions are your fortress for a daily healthy mindset. Pay attention to your present experience with openness, curiosity, and a willingness to be with "What is," which is the mindset of acceptance. This means accepting what you cannot change and taking steps to change what you can.

10 Steps to Manage Resentment

1. Quickly Manage This Emotion

Do not allow resentment to fester – it will only grow stronger if you do.

2. Learn to Identify the Underlying Emotion

Take the time to identify and embrace the deeper emotions that may be hiding beneath your anger, such as fear, hurt, or jealousy. Acknowledging these feelings can lead to greater understanding of the situation.

3. Emotional Vulnerability

Once you take the time to uncover the underlying cause of your resentment, allow yourself to fully engage with those powerful emotions. Accepting these feelings, along with the vulnerability they evoke, can lead to self-discovery and emotional healing. Embrace this introspection as a pathway to greater clarity and connection with yourself.

4. Communication Solves Most Problems

Engaging in open and heartfelt communication can be the key to overcoming many challenges. Whenever possible, take the time to articulate your emotions and thoughts to someone you trust. By sharing your feelings, you can initiate meaningful conversations that pave the way for prompt and constructive resolutions to your problems.

5. Prevent Judging or Labeling

When you let resentment surface and pass through you without the weight of labeling or harsh judgment, you create a space for growth. In doing so, you take ownership of your emotions, allowing yourself to approach them thoughtfully and manage them constructively once you recognize their presence.

6. Be Mentally Flexible

Rigid mindset is only strong until it breaks, a flexible attitude, on the other hand, is a powerful asset. It allows us to bend with the challenges we face, enabling us to understand and isolate issues effectively. By addressing problems without taking them personally, we maintain our strength and clarity in any situation. Embrace flexibility to enhance your resilience and problem-solving capabilities.

7. Embrace the Truth: We Are All Imperfect

Embrace the truth that every individual carries their own scars and flaws, including yourself. Recognizing this shared human experience harbors an environment where grace, mercy, and forgiveness flourish. These qualities enable you to go deeper into the emotions of others, allowing for genuine connections and understanding of their struggles.

8. Move On

It's important to recognize when it's time to move forward. Be brave enough to endure challenges for a higher purpose. Sometimes, letting go is the best path to the solution.

9. Identify Your Part

Embrace humility and take a moment to reflect on how you may have influenced the situation at hand. It is essential to acknowledge that, in many instances, our actions and choices play a significant role in the feelings of anger and resentment that arise. By understanding our contributions, we can address and resolve the underlying issues more effectively.

10. Self-Acceptance

Self-acceptance is the cornerstone for developing a growth mindset. It begins with recognizing that we are not perfect, making mistakes, and not needing to criticize ourselves every time we falter. Instead, it's important to accept the reality of what has occurred. This mindset helps prevent feelings of resentment and allows us to adapt and grow.

The Second "R": The Power of Resistance

This formidable force has the most power to affect your potential, often relegating you to the sidelines. When resistance takes hold, it can leave you feeling powerless, causing you to miss valuable opportunities in your life. My question is: How are you allowing resistance to hold you back?

Whenever you take a principled stand, face challenges, or strive to achieve something, you will encounter resistance. Resistance is also part of our emotional protection mechanism, which helps us assess situations and make decisions. It's one of the two bookends that influence the direction we decide to go or not go. Resistance is often quick to remind us of past decisions that didn't work out, but it has little to do with the reality of moving forward into the unknown. It continuously dwells in the background of our thoughts; it never goes away, and if left unchecked, it will derail your well-meaning efforts and leave you feeling like a failure.

In chapter 2, I emphasized the importance of addressing psychological resistance, which involves denying our true feelings and emotions. If you often find yourself complaining, feeling resentful, experiencing self-doubt, or struggling against your emotions, it's a sign that you're not fully embracing them. Resistance creates an invisible wall that separates your current self from the person you aspire to become. You can begin to dismantle this barrier by understanding and accepting your emotions. Recognizing and accepting these feelings is essential because they are fundamental to your identity. Our most powerful self is usually behind the strength of our resistance.

How do we minimize and manage resistance? First, we need to understand the power of this emotion. We must identify what triggers resistance and learn how to navigate it and break through the barriers that limit our capabilities. Resistance is a natural part of being human; it will always exist. However, recognizing and acknowledging it as it arises can equip us with strategies to overcome it.

Second, resistance is an inherent characteristic of change. It's also a physiological reaction to change. Our heart beats faster. Our mind starts to race. Public speaking is widely known to be a fear most people have. It creates tension in us. We worry about saying something wrong and embarrassing ourselves. If we speak in front of 10 people, the fear is noticeable. If we address a crowd of 100 people, the fear barometer increases. Why does speaking in front of a large group make us feel inadequate and unworthy? Psychologists or people in the neuroscience community will tell you that you need to understand your brain's prefrontal cortex to manage this resistance, which automates your thoughts, behavior, and actions. This is helpful intellectually but doesn't transcend into real-life experience and application.

The key to building a World-Class Mindset is learning not to resist yourself or allow others to get in the way of achieving your goals. We will examine two significant emotions that greatly influence our ability to cope with resistance: one may reinforce it, while the other can set us free.

Two Emotions That Cannot Coexist Simultaneously

When it comes to our emotional experiences, some feelings are fundamentally opposed to each other. For instance, you cannot feel pure happiness while being consumed by deep sadness at the same moment. Understanding this dynamic can help us navigate our emotions more effectively, allowing us to embrace the joy of life while recognizing the importance of processing our challenges separately. By acknowledging that certain emotions cannot coexist, we can gain clarity and find balance in our emotional well-being.

As discussed in chapter 2, fear represents the most significant barrier of resistance people encounter in sales. This resistance can manifest in various ways, such as procrastination, frustration, challenges, or fear of change, which can trigger these emotions.

Fear is often an exaggeration and distortion of our thoughts and feelings. Remember, it's never as bad as you think, and you are never as inadequate as you believe. Fear anticipates failure and causes us to worry about change, the unknown, and loss of control. It feeds our anxieties about death and tells us, "I can't," "You're not capable," or "You're not good enough." We worry about what others might think or say. It imagines the worst-case scenarios and thrives in our minds. "What ifs" appear through intimidation, anger, the need for control, stressful situations, and deadlines we must meet. Simply being alive can be a source of fear. Ultimately, fear occupies a significant space in our thinking and emotions.

This powerful mindset flourishes within a life of mediocrity, preventing us from living fully, achieving our dreams, trusting our instincts, and embracing failure. Resistance can hold us back from realizing our true potential and experiencing the meaningful accomplishments that life has to offer. Acquiring a mindset free from resistance and fear often contradicts our natural instincts. These emotions are deeply rooted beliefs that influence our ability to perform.

However, there is one primary emotion that surpasses the power of fear and cannot coexist with it: love. Love is the deepest emotional fabric of our being and embodies the essence of who God is. This gift is not crafted by human hands but instead a divine blessing. When you are spiritually awakened in the fullness of God's love, you gain the strength to rise above any earthly emotions that may impede your potential. This profound love instills in you a capability that transcends your own efforts and empowers you to achieve what once seemed unattainable.

You can break free from fear by embracing love as the center of your life. There is no greater force for eliminating resistance. A mindset grounded in love can dissolve barriers. In the sales world, radiating a loving presence allows you to forge deep connections with clients. When you convey love through your eyes and tone of voice while thoughtfully presenting your product, clients feel a sense of comfort and confidence in your commitment to quality service. By practicing love, we not only center our thoughts and feelings in truth and find strength, but we also unlock the potential to be our authentic selves, allowing us to be genuine in every interaction.

Love resonates with the deepest part of who we are and connects us with others. It renews and restores our inner harmony as every cell in our bodies tunes into this natural healing state. Focusing on love can retrain our brains to accept what we cannot change. Love helps us let go when resistance arises, allowing thoughts and feelings to pass without judgment. It is often said, "Happiness is a by-product of acceptance and change." Love enables us to accept "what is" and encourages us to move forward. It serves as a healing force that surpasses all other emotions. A World-Class Mindset thrives when it is anchored in love.

7 Steps to Manage Resistance

1. Identify What You Are Resisting

It will often show up through another emotion, like anger or procrastination. It could be because of a loss, a new beginning, a change in your life, etc. Once you can understand the root of your behavior, it will make change easier.

2. Accept It is a Normal Reaction

Recognize it's okay to experience resistance. It is a normal human reaction.

3. Adapting to Change

Adopt a learning mindset. One thing you can count on in life is that everything changes. Resisting change is resisting reality. The more you are in acceptance, the more powerful your mindset becomes.

4. Embrace Change

Embrace your power to manage change. All beliefs are choices and thoughts you have created. If you think change is difficult, it will be. If you begin to believe change is manageable, you are developing the mindset of acceptance.

5. Be Aware of the "What Ifs"

Be aware of the "What Ifs," "What if something terrible happens?" "What if it all goes wrong?" Each time, we ask ourselves, "What if?" We create an unbalanced view of the situation by focusing on negative scenarios, not positive possibilities.

6. Consider the Possibility

Ask yourself each time what the worst- and best-case scenario is in this situation. If you can live with either, you will overcome resistance and begin to move forward.

7. Be Proactive

Find activities or challenges you resist, such as public speaking, stating your opinion more often, leading others, etc. People only grow when they are challenged.

In closing, whenever you press through resistance, you exponentially grow in all other areas of your life. You begin trusting who you are and what you are capable of in any situation. A World-Class Mindset understands that risk rewards opportunity!

The Third "R": Revenge

Revenge is a destructive force that poses the greatest threat to our emotional state and the feelings of others. It wields a heavy influence, often leading individuals toward bitterness and resentment. This potent emotion can cloud our judgment, erode our sense of empathy, and develop a destructive mindset that ultimately damages relationships and personal growth.

Revenge is one of our deepest instincts. It has the power to seize our emotions and gain momentum over time. People seek revenge when they feel attacked, experience injustice, suffer hurt, face humiliation, or become victims of deceit, embarrassment, or mistreatment. It thrives in the shadows of vulnerability, where feelings of powerlessness linger. This impulse is not merely a reaction; it reflects a victim's mindset, rooted in resentment and the need for resistance. It is deeply personal, unpredictable, and proactive. Moreover, it can often spiral into a toxic mix of hate, jealousy, and envy, driven by the desire to deliver punishment. It relentlessly seeks satisfaction until it believes that justice has been served.

We've all had that intense rush of anger while driving, a moment when another driver recklessly cuts us off, igniting a flare of indignation. In that instant, we might think, "I hope they get what they deserve!" This emotional turmoil compels us to accelerate, our hearts racing with a mix of frustration and a craving for retribution. Have you ever paused to reflect on how many people are incarcerated today because of the destructive force of revenge? These overwhelming feelings can spark a wildfire of vengeance within us, tainting our thoughts and skewing our ability to make rational decisions. A striking line from the iconic movie *Dirty Harry*, where he defiantly declares, "Go ahead, make my day," perfectly encapsulates that intoxicating rush we feel when anger pushes us toward adopting a vengeful mindset. It is imperative to examine how powerful this emotion can shape our mindset, have significant and far-reaching consequences, and impact our lives and well-being.

The Problem When This Emotion Is Engaged

The real challenge arises when this deep-rooted inclination to seek retribution is ignited. Confucius wisely observed, "Before you embark on a journey of revenge, dig two graves!" This poignant phrase serves as a stark warning, illustrating that the path of vengeance leads to the downfall of the intended target and often results in the destruction of the avengers themselves.

How many times have we seen a player give a cheap shot, but the ref only sees the retaliation of the second player and throws him out of the game? Was it fair? No, but revenge works this way. It always leaves you holding the short end of the stick. It has the same effect when you gossip or inflict emotional stress on another person you want to hurt. If you act upon revenge, you will pay a higher price.

You do not need to act on revenge for people to be affected. The damage is in your mind. It affects your attitude. You might find yourself grappling with feelings of anger, impatience, or even a short temper. These emotions often stem from a deeper desire for revenge. It's important to recognize how these feelings play a role in shaping your overall mindset. Revenge will sideline logic, decisively compromise your judgment, and impair your ability to act decisively in any situation. Many individuals experience feelings of revenge that can remain suppressed for extended periods, days, weeks, or even years. Allowing this emotion to take hold will diminish your potential and embed it into your core mindset. Every time you slip into the revenge mindset, even subtly, you surrender your power and shift into a victim mentality. This transition allows outside influences to dictate your emotions and behaviors. Refuse to let revenge control you; instead, reclaim your strength and focus on what truly matters.

Feelings of revenge can strike suddenly and manifest in various ways. Experiencing these feelings is a natural part of being human. However, the key lies in recognizing when these vengeful thoughts begin to surface and learning to observe them without becoming entangled, allowing yourself to be dragged along by the powerful train of revenge as it departs the station. People with a World-Class Mindset can insulate themselves from this emotional poison. Choosing instead a path of inner strength and emotional well-being.

4 Steps to Manage Revenge

1. Take A Full Day Away

Take a full day away when you feel a sense of revenge. The further you get from the offense, the more objective you can be in assessing the situation.

2. Identify the Offense

Identify the underlying feeling of the offense. Is it envy, an insult, a loss, mistreatment, or situational? Once you can identify what it is, you can better manage it.

3. Communicate Your Experience

Remember that even though you may be tempted to play judge and jury, you only punish yourself. If the conflict is with someone you know, communicate your experience, and allow their character to show up. If it doesn't, you know your side of the street is clean, and you can move on.

4. Forgive When You Can

Seek forgiveness when you can. We are all working with broken people. A World-Class Mindset does not allow any offense to dent their armor. They understand we are all human. Everyone falls short.

Summarizing The 3 R's

The three greatest rationalizers and neutralizers of a World-Class Mindset are Resentment, Resistance, and Revenge. These three have a profound impact on how we perform in life. What makes these emotions so destructive is that they are constant. Without realizing it, these emotions may last for years or a lifetime. When we allow them to influence our thinking, they interfere with our potential and hinder our ability to perform our best. If we stay in this mindset, they relentlessly sustain destructive thoughts. These are the most potent negative emotions you can carry. These emotions will poison your physical and mental health, destroy joy and happiness, and remove your ability to be the best "You." Remember, you are the product in sales.

These emotions prevent you from building world-class mental strength because it allows you to be a victim. It creates an excuse not to take responsibility, absolves us from the painful necessity to change, and then insulates us from the possibility of failure. It is the perfect excuse to be a failure! No one would argue you may be justified for having these emotions. All of us have been in relationships with people we believe are responsible for the anger, abuse, hurt, and loss we feel. But we must decide whether to continue to be controlled by these thoughts and feelings or move on.

You will get emotionally punched, cut, bruised, and battered at times, figuratively speaking. But if you cannot move on, you are disarming the power of your mindset. Be aware when self-defeating emotions enter your life. Let negative emotions pass without judgment, allowing positive feelings to take root and grow. Allow yourself to process your emotions, but do not allow them to steal your power. You have lost control if you stop taking responsibility and become a victim. Stay alert to the underlying strength of the 3 Rs. Remember, people with a World-Class Mindset can solve challenges by managing their thoughts regardless of the outcome or circumstances they find themselves in.

The 3 R's Sales Questionnaire

Instructions: Rate your agreement with each statement below using the following scale: Be honest—this is about self-awareness, not perfection.

1 = Never (0%)
2 = Rarely (less than 25%)
3 = Sometimes (about 50%)
4 = Often (about 75%)
5 = Always (100%)

Section 1: Resentment

1.	I hold onto disappointment when a deal falls through unexpectedly.	
2.	I feel underappreciated for how hard I work in sales.	
3.	I find it difficult to celebrate colleagues' wins if I'm underperforming.	
4.	I revisit past client interactions that made me feel disrespected.	
5.	I sometimes think clients "owe me" for the effort I put in.	
6.	I internalize negative feedback more than I'd like to admit.	
7.	When I've been overlooked or micromanaged, I carry that feeling forward.	
8.	I compare myself to peers in a way that leaves me frustrated.	
9.	I feel like management favors other reps, regardless of performance.	
10.	I replay conversations in my head to prove I was right.	

Section 2: Resistance

11.	I procrastinate on outreach after being rejected.	
12.	I avoid certain types of prospects or industries because they "don't get me."	
13.	I default to "it won't work anyway" thinking during sales lulls.	
14.	I dread weekly pipeline reviews or performance check-ins.	
15.	I resist using new tools or processes, even if they could help.	
16.	I delay emotionally difficult conversations with clients or managers.	
17.	I hesitate to ask for help even when I know I need support.	
18.	I talk myself out of bold ideas before I try them.	
19.	I find excuses to avoid things that might improve my sales habits.	
20.	I overexplain setbacks instead of owning and adjusting.	

Section 3: Revenge

21.	I withhold effort when I feel a client is being rude or difficult.	
22.	I disconnect from team participation when my input is dismissed.	
23.	I let deals "die" without full follow-through if I feel the prospect isn't respectful.	
24.	I mentally check out in meetings where I don't feel heard or valued.	
25.	I withhold helpful advice or feedback from coworkers I don't get along with.	
26.	I feel tempted to "prove a point" by letting someone fail.	
27.	I disengage when I feel invisible to leadership.	
28.	I try to sound agreeable but secretly enjoy when someone struggles after ignoring my idea.	
29.	I focus more on being "right" than being helpful.	
30.	I sometimes fantasize about leaving a client or team member hanging to teach them a lesson.	

Scoring: (Total Possible Score: 30–150)

Add up your total score	

Score 30–60 / Clear Channel - You're emotionally agile. You're grounded.

It's not just the absence of baggage; it's the presence of real-time emotional discipline and forward-focused clarity. Setbacks don't stick to you; they shape you. You feel disappointment without turning it into bitterness. You absorb feedback without letting it corrode your confidence. In conversation, your energy is clean: clients feel heard, not pushed. Teammates feel supported, not judged. You act from presence, not past resentment. Being a "clear channel" means that emotional friction doesn't get passed along. This doesn't mean you suppress emotion; it means you process, integrate, and let go faster than most. And that's a leadership skill few ever master.

Score 61–90 / Occasional Static - Most of the time, you operate with clarity and positive intent. You listen, respond, and show up with integrity. However, under situational stress, such as tight deadlines, emotional objections, ego-triggering feedback, or competitive comparison, your signal can become scrambled. It's not overt resentment or outright disengagement; it's a subtle interference in your presence, confidence, or commitment. Past frustrations linger beneath the surface: maybe a deal that felt unfair, a recognition gap, or internal politics that dented your sense of significance. These unresolved feelings leak into your interactions. The goal isn't to eliminate pressure; it's to become more signal than static, even when the volume gets turned up.

Score 91–115 / Internal Interference - Underneath the activity, there's emotional static, resentment about unspoken slights, resistance to processes you don't believe in, or subtle revenge behaviors like withholding effort or energy. This isn't sabotage in the traditional sense, it's erosion. And it shows up in small ways: What is the impact? Your connection feels off. Prospects may sense less empathy. Your consistency dips; you move more reactively, less rhythmically.

And your conviction wavers. You say the words, but the weight behind them is thinner. This isn't about fault. It's about emotional debt and choosing whether to carry it or clear it.

Score 116–150 / Toxic Loop -*You may be stuck in recurring emotional patterns that start with a trigger—like a rejection, a micromanaging manager, an underwhelming team dynamic and spiral into self-limiting behavior: Toxic Loop isn't just an emotional glitch, it's a behavioral cycle that repeats because something inside you hasn't been seen, healed, or redefined. When left unchecked, it distorts connection, weakens performance, and chips away at how you view yourself. At first, it feels protective. Later, it becomes punishment. The loop steals energy, erodes trust (from others and yourself), and puts a ceiling on your impact—not because you aren't capable, but because part of you doesn't want to fully commit until the emotional ledger is clean. This isn't a mindset issue, it's an identity conflict: "Can I be fully myself in this environment and still be safe, successful, and seen?"*

CHAPTER 10
MAGNA MINDSET OVERVIEW
"ELITE ISN'T A PERSONALITY, IT'S A PRACTICE" - BRUCE DANIELSON

At the beginning of this book, we asked the question, "What is a World-Class Mindset?" We explored its importance, outlined practical steps to achieve it, and discussed the significant impact it can have on both our personal and professional lives. We also discovered that 70% to 80% of salespeople fail within their first 1 to 3 years. Now, let's revisit each chapter to reinforce the key insights you've gained on your transformative journey to developing a World-Class Mindset in sales and life, ensuring you feel prepared and confident for the path ahead.

Chapter 1 - Evaluate Your Mindset

We began managing and evaluating your mindset, strengths, and weaknesses. We looked at how moving from a fixed to a growth mindset is the foundation of a World-Class Mindset. This mindset is rooted in the belief that sales skills and emotional intelligence are not fixed but can be developed. This shift is essential as it lays the groundwork for producing a World-Class Mindset that empowers you to reach new heights and achieve extraordinary success.

Chapter 2 - Resistance, Fear and Failure

We embraced a proactive approach to overcoming the psychological barriers that can hinder success in sales. By acknowledging and embracing our emotions, like fear, failure, and resistance, we discovered the power of allowing these feelings to flow through us instead of battling them. This transformative process promotes personal growth and resilience and empowers us to tackle challenges head-on and confidently achieve our sales goals.

Chapter 3 - World-Class Mental Toughness

We thoroughly explored the constructive concept of mental toughness, emphasizing its significant role in achieving personal and professional success, particularly in the competitive sales landscape. Understanding why this strength is essential is a pivotal step toward growth. We identified actionable strategies to cultivate it effectively. By developing mental determination, you can build a resilient mindset that helps you overcome challenges and harness opportunities for advancement and success, ensuring you are well-prepared for the demands of the sales industry.

Chapter 4 - World-Class Emotional Intelligence

We actively pursued techniques to enhance our self-awareness, a key factor in understanding and identifying our emotions. This has also made us more attuned to the feelings of others in the sales environment. By sharpening these emotional insights, we can build deeper connections with clients, ultimately leading to more successful outcomes in our sales endeavors and strengthening our client relationships.

Chapter 5 - World-Class Attitude

We explored the mindset necessary for a world-class attitude. This type of attitude is a God-given trait rooted in self-awareness. It enables you to assess situations accurately and guides you through challenges and adversity. When used effectively, your potential is only limited by the power of your attitude. Let it inspire and empower you and avoid personalizing failure or allowing it to become part of your identity. A sustained, positive attitude always looks for the next opportunity, even when things go wrong. While it is natural to experience negative emotions, we cannot stop them but choose where to direct our attention. Our focus is best directed toward finding the next solution!

Chapter 6 - World-Class Responsibility

We found a World-Class Mindset cannot develop without embracing responsibility. When we fail to take ownership and instead blame others or see ourselves as victims, we risk losing the trust and confidence of those around us. On the other hand, each time you take responsibility for your actions, you not only strengthen your mental resilience but also experience personal growth. The more responsibility you are willing to accept, the more confidence and personal power you will develop in various areas of your life, including your relationships, sales performance, and overall experiences.

Chapter 7 - The Power of NOW

We focused on effective time management; a World-Class Mindset thrives in the power of "NOW." When you are fully centered in the present moment; you unleash your potential and reach the pinnacle of productivity. By structuring your day around the Power of the Hour, you systematically divide your work into intentional one-hour segments, each centered around a specific objective. This strategy eliminates distractions, allowing you to hone in on your tasks with unwavering focus.

As you embrace this practice, you'll notice a transformation in how you manage your time and effort, resulting in a deeper sense of determination and clarity as you methodically work through your to-do list. Embrace the power of living in the moment to discover your highest capabilities!

Chapter 8 - Authentic Enthusiasm

We've learned that authentic enthusiasm is a powerful force that not only energizes your sales and life but also deeply impacts your prospects. It's an invaluable personal quality that invigorates and inspires your prospects as you share your message. When you passionately share your excitement for a product, it captivates and motivates your prospects. Picture the difference between a flat, monotonal delivery and the rich, immersive experience of stereo sound that enhances the experience of beautiful music. By authentically conveying your passion and clearly illustrating the benefits your product offers, your prospects will feel that infectious energy and be inspired to take action.

Chapters 9 - The Power of the 3 R's

We recognized the impact of three cataclysmic supernovas on our negative emotions: Resentment, Resistance, and Revenge. These feelings are among the greatest rationalizers and neutralizers of our mindset. They profoundly affect our performance in life. However, one transformative force is more powerful than these gravitational death stars: the power of a World-Class Mindset. When practiced and maintained, this mindset helps you stay grounded in your mental strengths. It is a commitment and a dedication to your personal growth. Unlocks your true potential, guiding you toward remarkable achievements.

THE FINAL TRANSFORMATION OF YOUR MINDSET

Early on in this book, I asked you to open a new room in your mind, a space that you have never entered before, and I asked you throughout these chapters to emotionally move into and trust the principles in this room, the old you cannot enter this space.

You now have the foundation of:

The strength of a **Growth Mindset**
5 steps to manage **Resistance, Fear, and Failure**
10 steps to strengthen **World-Class Mental Toughness**
10 steps in maintaining a **World-Class Attitude**
8 principles to increase **World-Class Emotional Intelligence**
10 principles of **World-Class Responsibility**
3 steps to harness the **The Power of NOW**
3 steps to grow **Authentic Enthusiasm.**
10 steps to manage **Resentment - #1 (3 R's)**
7 steps to manage **Resistance - #2 (3 R's)**
4 steps to manage **Revenge - #3 (3 R's)**

THE FINAL TRANSFORMATION OF YOUR MINDSET

Now is the time to turn around and close the door on your old emotions and thinking. Do not look back! This is the new you! Practice staying in this new space, these principles will transform the fundamental character traits of your behavior, thinking, attitude, beliefs, work ethic, and sales ability. You have retrained your mind to have a deep-seated knowledge and understanding of the mindset of world-class producers.

Your income and sales skill set will dramatically increase if you stay, live, and operate from this mindset. Opening your mindset to these principles is the power that produces these results. There is no greater gift you can give yourself and others around you, and there is no other change you could make that would impact, empower, and accelerate your success immediately.

When you integrate and practice these principles, they become a habit in your life and business. You are practicing the mindset of world-class thinking in sales. Your life will produce world-class results.

You now have the tools to join the elite 1%.

I wish you the best!

"Elite Isn't a Personality - It's a Practice"
Bruce Danielson
Performance Based Development Author/Speaker/CEO

ABOUT THE AUTHOR

Bruce is a top 1% producer, mindset strategist, and a pioneer in sales psychology with over three decades of elite frontline performance. His journey is living proof that Mindset isn't a buzzword, it's the engine behind extraordinary results. Known for turning raw self-awareness into high-impact, practical tools, Bruce has spent decades decoding the invisible patterns that separate high achievers from the average. His methods combine real-world sales expertise with profound psychological insight, enabling professionals to overcome internal resistance and operate with clarity, conviction, and velocity.

In his debut book, *Magna Mindset: The Elite Mindset of World-Class Producers*, Bruce unveils a transformative framework that guides readers from hesitation to elite execution. It's not a collection of tactics, it's a roadmap for becoming the kind of person who naturally produces excellence. With powerful step-by-step models and emotional clarity, Bruce helps readers replace self-doubt with alignment, urgency, and inner authority.

Below are some of Bruce's accomplishments over the years:

- 1987 - New Horizons Computer Learning – National Sales Executive - Elite 1%
- 1995 - Mega Life - National Rookie of The Year
- 1997 - Fortis/Assurant - Elite 1% National Producer
- 2002 - National Training Director (Largest IMO in U.S.)
- 2005 - Assurant Life - Elite 1% National Producer
- 2009 - American General - Elite 1% National Producer
- 2014 - Mutual of Omaha - Elite 1% National Producer
- 2017 - Phoenix Life - Elite 1% National Producer
- 2020 - National Life - Elite 1% National Producer
- 2023 - Trainer, Speaker, and Author of *Magna Mindset – The Elite Mindset of World-Class Producers* and CEO of the Magna Mindset Training System

For more information about Bruce and his
Magna Mindset Training System
visit his website below:

https://magnamindsettraining.com

www.ingramcontent.com/pod-product-compliance
Lightning Source LLC
Chambersburg PA
CBHW060657100426
42734CB00047B/2010